W9-BFQ-639

The Good Dog Library

Train Your Dog Right

Basic Obedience, Skill Building & Problem Solving

ISBN: 1-879-620-66-9

Belvoir Publications Inc.
Box 2626
75 Holly Hill Lane
Greenwich, CT 06836 USA

Train Your Dog Right: Basic Obedience, Skill Building & Problem Solving
The editors of Your Dog and Whole Dog Journal

ISBN: 1-879-620-66-9
1. Dogs-Training 2. Canine 3. Canine Training

Manufactured in the United States of America

The Good Dog Library

Train Your Dog Right

Basic Obedience, Skill Building & Problem Solving

Edited by Diane L. Muhlfeld

Belvoir Publications, Inc.
Greenwich, CT

Contents

Section III: Problem-Specific Training

Section IV: Training Tools

Preface

You've finally brought your tumbling bundle of fur home from the breeder or the pound—and now what? Well, now begins the fun—and work—of integrating these cute, squirmy beings into our families and society. No matter their age—and current findings indicate the younger, the better—dog training should begin almost immediately after you bring your new pet home.

If you're a reader of Whole Dog Journal, or Your Dog, you already know we advocate positive reinforcement training—extensive use of Click! and encouraging, simple words backed up by special treats. The goal is to get our canine pals to do what we want them to—voluntarily. And while it's not as difficult as you might think, training takes commitment, time and patience, sometimes a variety of tools—crates, special collars, leashes—and myriad techniques (even one based on, yes, training chickens).

In Volume Two of The Good Dog Library, Train Your Dog Right: Basic Obedience, Skill Building & Problem Solving, we're going to cover the broad spectrum of training-related information starting with what medium best suits you—group classes? Private Trainer? Print? Video? And we'll take you through the principles of "operant conditioning," an umbrella phrase that teaches cause and effect: an association between a behavior and its consequence, along with other training theories. We'll take you through the all important first command —"Come, Now"—that could mean the difference between life and death for your pup, and we'll show you how to get your dog's attention (most important!) and how to train your dog while you're playing together.

We'll also introduce you to a variety of training possibilities that go beyond "Sit" and "Stay" and "Heel"— agility training, herding, flyball, even dancing with your dog, commonly known as "musical freestyle." We profile four trainers who bring an almost professorial intellect to their training theories and techniques reflecting their lifelong dedication to the field.

And we'll address the best way to handle special problems that socially unskilled dogs sometimes have—how to recognize and head off impending aggression, what to do if your dog is noise-phobic or, worse, a biter, how to handle a timid dog or the opposite, a jumper.

The whole goal of training is to integrate our special animal friends into our worlds so we can coexist happily, bringing to each other the best of both breeds—theirs and ours.

Diane L. Muhlfeld
Greenwich, CT
June 2000

Section I

Basic Training

1

Choosing the Right Training Medium

Print? Video? Cyberspace? Live and in Person? Solo or Group? Your choices are legion.

Today there are more dog-training options than ever before. In addition to group and private classes, you can choose from hundreds of books, reams of magazine articles, dozens of videos, and even dog-training sites on the web. But which medium suits you and Bowser best?

Clarifying your objectives can help you decide which instructional tool to select. If you've never trained a dog before and want to teach your pooch to obey the indispensable "Sit," "Stay," and "Come" commands, a basic-obedience class might be most useful.

If you're training your dog for competition—either in obedience or one of the many canine working or athletic events—you'll probably benefit from the extra help that subject-specific books and videos provide.

If you are seeking to solve minor canine foibles such as pulling on lead or jumping, any instructional tool—properly selected and applied—can help. However, solving more serious behavior problems such as separation anxiety or aggression may require one-on-one sessions with a qualified trainer or animal behaviorist.

Another important criterion for selecting a training tool is the trainer's philosophy. No matter which training tool you choose, make sure the techniques emphasize positive reinforcement (such as praise and play) rather than punishment. "That way, you'll have a dog that wants to work for you rather than a dog that's afraid of you," notes Dr. Linda Aronson, a veterinary behavioral consultant in Lexington,

Massachusetts. If you disagree with the trainer's approach, don't buy the book or video or sign up for the class. Also, avoid trainers or training materials that promise quick fixes.

Print, Video, or Cyberspace?

As you're mulling over training-media options, keep in mind that every training vehicle has both pluses and minuses. Videos show you techniques in action, and you can rewind tapes repeatedly to review specific material.

Videos are also useful if you and your pooch need to brush up on previously learned skills. But before investing in a training video, consider whether the medium fits your personal learning style. If you've learned successfully from cooking or skiing videos, try a dog-training video. But if your instructional videos collect dust atop the VCR, consider a book or a class.

With books, it's easy to know what you're getting before you buy. Unlike videos, where you're usually at the mercy of promotional blurbs on the covers, books give you the freedom to thumb through and see what's inside. Also, most books contain more information than will fit into a single video script. Books are also more portable than videos.

As for the Web, a word of caution: Anyone can post information on the Web, so check out the informant's qualifications before using any methods you find in cyberspace.

Live and In Person: Your Best Bet

Although books and videos can be helpful dog-training adjuncts, there's nothing like a class with a competent trainer. A trainer can watch you working with your dog, tailor techniques to fit both you and your dog, and answer your questions.

Classes also give Bowser a chance to socialize with other dogs—a vital element in canine behavioral development. The presence of other dogs and people also provides real-life distractions that help test the skills your dog is learning.

Plus, knowing that you both have to "perform" each week in front of a group may motivate you to work more diligently with Bowser on your own—a key to training success.

But dog training classes vary widely in style and quality of instruction. It is important to do research and make an informed choice before selecting a trainer. Before putting your dog's future in a trainer's hands, we recommend that you ask a lot of questions. Look for a trainer who has had experience handling hundreds or thousands of dogs, and who has taught classes for at least two years. There are very few reputable dog trainer certification programs. While ongoing education is vital for a professional trainer, a brief certification course cannot provide a would-be trainer with the necessary experience brought by years of dog handling and training.

Find out where she got her training. Her combined experiences should total at least several years of exposure to a variety of breeds and mixture of breeds. Find out what other activities are available, if not through her, then through other trainers and dog clubs in the area. Ask if her training methods will prepare you for the other activities that capture your interest.

When you find the style that appeals to you, watch a class before you enroll. Dogs and owners should appear to be enjoying themselves; if they aren't, you probably won't either.

Make sure you like the methods the trainer uses. If you see something that makes you uncomfortable, a harsh punishment, for example, ask the trainer after the class whether what you witnessed is par for her course. She might regard the method as "necessary" for most dogs — or a rare occurrence she felt forced to try after failing with other methods. Trust your instincts about her response.

Investigating Instructors

Since there are no universal certification standards, academic-degree requirements, or licensing regulations, anyone can call him- or herself a "dog trainer." So how do you select a reputable instructor?

- *Seek references from dog-owning friends, your veterinarian, or your local humane society.*

- *Personally investigate a trainer's techniques by auditing a class without your dog.*

- *Watch all participants. If you see angry, frustrated people and cowering canines, look elsewhere.*

- *Look for a trainer who gives individualized attention and tailors training methods to fit different types of dogs and people.*

You Get What You Pay For

Be cautious of classes offered by dog clubs and large chain pet stores. They are often less expensive than those taught at privately owned dog training schools, but they are also frequently taught by their members, who may or may not have any previous teaching experience. These classes are often large, with little individual attention given. Also, many club classes use force-based training only. Chain pet stores may advertise positive reinforcement, but often hire novice trainers with little or no training knowledge or experience. They also tend to have a high turnover, since quality trainers can do better on their own.

The cost of dog training can vary widely. Free courses can sometimes be found through clubs or city recreation departments (just remember, you get what you pay for). Group classes that meet once a week can range from as little as $45 to $125 or more for a six- to eight-week course. (The price generally reflects cost of living in the area.) Expect an average of six to eight people and their dogs in the class; larger classes should have assistant trainers to help the trainer offer each of the students at least a little individual attention. This type of multi-week course is almost always paid for in advance.

Many trainers also offer private instruction at their school or, sometimes, at your home. Expect to pay from $45 to $150 an hour for this type of one-on-one session. During a one-hour consultation for a specific behavior challenge, your trainer should

Knowing that you both have to "perform" each week in front of a group may motivate you to work more diligently with Bowser on your own—a key to training success.

demonstrate one or more approaches for resolving the behavior and watch you apply the techniques. You can also expect her to offer options for an ongoing training program for you and your dog.

Going to Class

Once you select a trainer, but before you attend the first class, try to have a brief discussion with the person in charge. Make sure he or she is aware of your goal for the class, to prevent any misunderstandings regarding the intensity (or lack thereof!) with which you pursue perfection in your dog.

First, though, you have to decide what you want from a training class. Class styles vary, with the two primary approaches being the military-style precision training traditionally used for showing in the obedience ring, and family dog classes that are more concerned with teaching canine good manners and social skills.

The easiest way to tell the difference between the two is to ask what equipment is required. If the answer is "a choke chain, slip collar, training collar, or prong collar," the class is probably the more formal obedience class that relies on the use of force and physical correction. If the answer is "a flat buckle collar or a headcollar," you have found the more relaxed family dog class that uses positive reinforcement, rewards (treats) and praise—rather than jerks on a collar—to train the dog.

Finally, remember, practicing at home needn't be drudgery. "Once you know the basic techniques, you can use everyday interactions—such as feeding, grooming, and playing—as opportunities to reinforce training," concludes Dr. Aronson

And don't hesitate to excuse yourself and walk out of a class if you are told to do something to your dog that makes you feel uncomfortable. It can be difficult and embarrassing to disagree with a trainer, especially in front of an entire class full of her devotees, but remember, it's your relationship with your dog and his trust in you that is important, not someone else's opinion. There will always be another class and another day to get it right.

Trainers and classes vary in focus, intensity, and cost. Be sure to find an environment that you and your dog enjoy.

2

Different Strokes

Training techniques are many and varied. We can help you choose the right approach for your dog.

One sunny summer day, you're taking a stroll around the neighborhood. You pass a park and notice a dog training class in progress. The instructor is standing in a meadow with a number of dogs and owners circling her. Each of the dogs is wearing a shiny chain collar. From time to time when a dog forges ahead or lags behind, the owner jerks on the leash to bring the dog back to heel position, then pets and praises it. You hear an occasional "No!" issued in a commanding tone. The dogs appear well-behaved, and all of them are doing the same thing at precisely the same time.

You continue on, and reach another park where you see another training class. This is a more ragged-looking bunch, although also well-behaved. A half-dozen dogs are walking in different directions with their owners, turning, stopping and starting up again apparently at random. The dogs are wearing regular flat collars. Some of them also wear something around their noses that looks like a muzzle, but on closer inspection you realize it is more like a horse halter. There is no jerking, but there is much treat-tossing and talking; you hear a lot of "Yes!" and an occasional, odd, clicking noise. Since you have been thinking about signing your dog up for training, you pause to ponder the differences between the two groups.

Both groups are beginning dog training classes. Both can produce well-trained dogs. The main differences are the training methods and the philosophies and behavior theories behind those methods.

The Training Continuum

All dog training techniques fit somewhere on a continuum, from seriously harsh and abusive punishment-based methods at one extreme, to pure positive reinforcement at the other. Neither extreme is likely to be very practical or effective, nor will you find many trainers who recommend using only methods from one extreme or the other. Most trainers use a combination of techniques that place them somewhere between the two ends of the continuum. Which side of center trainers are on defines them as primarily compulsion-based or primarily positive-based.

Within the dog training community the debate about methods is generally good-natured, albeit spirited. Hackles get raised when trainers, who tend to be an opinionated lot, disagree on the very best method to resolve a particular canine behavior challenge.

Why the diversity in training protocol? Because there are, in fact, numerous training approaches that can successfully teach a dog to do what we ask, and because people bring an infinite number of philosophical, cultural, emotional, and ideological differences to the dog training profession.

Variety is the spice of life, it's true, but the number and variety of training styles available can make things a little confusing when you go looking for a trainer or an obedience class for your new dog. Would you have any idea what an instructor meant if she told you that her program was all about "positive punishment and compulsion training?" Or if another trainer told you that he teaches only "clicker training?"

What follows will provide you with definitions for these terms, and more. Armed with this glossary, you'll be able to "talk training" with people from all schools of canine behavior modification, and find a class format that works best for your and your dog.

Behavioral Theories

In behavioral terms, training is known as "conditioning behavior." We really aren't teaching our dog any new behaviors when we train. She already knows how to sit, lie down, stay in one place, walk by our side, or come running to us from far away – when she wants to. She just may not know how to do it (or may not choose to do it) when we ask her to. Training is conditioning (or teaching) the dog to reliably give us the behaviors we ask for, when we ask for them.

Classical conditioning

As first described by Pavlov, there is an association between a stimulus and a response, or behavior. (A stimulus is something that elicits a response.) This is the famous "ring a bell, the dog salivates," experiment that most of us learned about in high school psychology classes. Classical conditioning can generally be used to teach only very simple behaviors.

Operant conditioning

This method is most commonly used for training, because it can be used to teach complex behaviors and behavior "chains," a series of behaviors strung together. With operant conditioning there is an association between a behavior and its consequence. The dog does something, then something happens as a result of the dog's behavior. There are four ways that this works. Two are labeled "positive," which means, in this usage, that the dog's behavior makes something appear. Two are labeled "negative," which means the dog's behavior makes something go away. The "something" may be pleasant or unpleasant, but it is not necessarily what the terms "positive" and "negative" refer to, as the following explains.

- Positive reinforcement: The dog's behavior makes something good happen. For example, when the dog walks next to you without pulling on the leash, she gets a treat (treat = good thing).
- Positive punishment: The dog's behavior makes something bad happen. Example: If the dog pulls on the leash, her neck gets jerked to bring her back to heel position (jerk on neck = bad thing).
- Negative punishment: The dog's behavior makes something good go away. Example: When the treat is used as a lure to keep the dog walking in heel position, she may jump up to get it. The treat is hidden until she stops jumping. Every time she jumps up the treat is hidden, until she stays on the ground as the treat is offered (treat = good thing; hidden = "goes away").
- Negative reinforcement: The dog's behavior makes something bad go away. Example: A no-pull harness puts pressure on the dog's chest as long as the dog puts pressure on the leash. When the dog stops pulling, the pressure stops. (pressure = bad thing; no pulling = bad thing "goes away").

Compulsion Training

Traditional, compulsion-based training works on the philosophy that we have to show the dog who is boss. She must do what we say, and quickly. If she doesn't, we immediately correct her or she will learn that she can ignore our commands. The primary tool for compulsion trainers is positive punishment (the dog's behavior makes something bad happen, like a jerk on the leash), often followed by a treat, a pat, and/or verbal praise to keep up the dog's enthusiasm for the training process. Twenty years ago the use of food treats as praise was abhorrent to traditional trainers.

Compulsion training works, as demonstrated by decades of well-behaved dogs. Proponents argue that the small amount of discomfort that the dogs experience is worth the end result of a reliable, promptly responsive dog, and skilled trainers use the minimum amount of force necessary to get the job done. But this approach can be problematic with very dominant or independent dogs who don't take kindly to being pushed and pulled around and may decide to argue back. In this case, a person taking this approach must be prepared to use enough force to get their message across quickly, and be willing to escalate the level of force if necessary. Potentially dangerous techniques like "scruff shakes" and "alpha rolls" work only if the trainer is strong enough to persevere if the dog fights back. Many owners and trainers are either unwilling or unable to use this kind of force with their dogs.

Advocates of compulsion-based training argue that the small amount of discomfort that a dog experiences is worth the result—a reliable, promptly responsive dog.

Timid, submissive or sensitive dogs may also not do well with positive punishment. Forceful corrections can cause them to "melt down," and miscalculations can cause damage to the owner's or trainer's relationship with the dog.

Yet another concern about compulsion training is the possible damage to a dog's throat from a standard choke chain collar, which can exert tremendous pressure on a dog's trachea. They are not recommended for puppies under the age of six months, yet it is more and more widely accepted that starting puppies in training classes at the age of 10 weeks is ideal, in order to take advantage of a pup's critical socialization and learning period. Prong collars reputedly distribute the pressure more evenly around the neck and are less likely to do damage, but many owners understandably shy away from using the medieval looking spikes on their tender baby puppies.

Clicker Training

"Clicker trainers" is a slang term for individuals who use positive reinforcement as their first training method of choice, combined with an **audible signal** to indicate the desired behavior. These trainers operate on a different training philosophy from the compulsion trainers, preferring to get the dog to offer the desired behavior voluntarily, then mark and reward it when it does. (The **marker signal**, or "bridge," can be the Click! of the clicker, a whistle, some other mechanical sound, or a word. "Yes!" is frequently used to mark a correct behavior.) Behaviors that are ignored (not rewarded) tend to go away, or "extinguish." Since all living creatures tend to repeat behaviors that are rewarding, behaviors that are repeatedly marked and rewarded by a dog's owner get offered more and more frequently.

Take, for example, the puppy who wants to jump up on everyone. Dogs greet each other face-to-face, so it is natural for our dogs to want to greet our faces. Plus, when they are cute little puppies we pick them up and cuddle them in our arms, thereby rewarding them for being "up." Small wonder that so many dogs jump on people!!

Many of the suggested compulsion approaches to correcting jumping behavior actually reward the very behavior we are trying to extinguish. When the dog jumps up, she touches us. That's a reward. We look at her. Eye contact is a reward. We speak to her to tell her to get off. We are paying attention to her—that's a reward! We reach down to push her away. We touched her—another reward!! For some rowdy dogs, even the time-honored "knee her in the chest" is an invitation to start a rousing game of body-slam.

The positive reinforcement approach (the dog's behavior makes something good happen) relies on the principle that behaviors that are ignored will extinguish. But how do you ignore an enthusiastic canine who is leaping up to greet you nose-to-nose, inflicting multiple bruises and lacerations in the process? Just standing still doesn't work; she gets all kinds of self-rewards by jumping all over you.

Instead, we turn our back on the dog and step away. As the dog tries to come around to face us, we do it again. Turn away and step away, over and over. Sooner or later (and with most dogs this happens much sooner than you would imagine) the dog gets frustrated and confused, and sits down to puzzle out your bizarre behavior. Bingo! Now you turn toward her, tell her "Yes!" and feed her the treat from the stash you keep in your pockets in anticipation of opportunities just like this. You can also pet her and praise her. If she jumps up again, repeat the process. The theory goes that before you know it, she will have figured out that in order to get the attention she craves as quickly as possible, she needs to sit when she approaches you, not jump.

Actually, the latter approach also uses negative punishment: the dog's behavior (jumping up) causes something good (you) to go away. Then, when she sits and you give her a treat and attention, it is positive reinforcement—the dog's behavior (sitting) causes something good (treat and attention) to happen.

Years ago using a treat as a reward or incentive was frowned upon by many trainers. Today, the method is widely accepted.

Clicker trainers use primarily positive reinforcement, but will also use varying degrees of negative punishment, negative reinforcement and positive punishment, depending on the dog and the individual trainer's own comfort level and skill with the various methods.

Proponents of positive reinforcement training claim that a training approach based on rewards rather than punishment builds trust in the human-canine relationship and encourages the dog to think for herself and freely make deliberate choices of rewardable behavior rather than living in fear of being punished for making a wrong choice. Proponents of the approach state that dogs trained with these methods tend to be more willing to think for themselves, choose "right" behaviors, take risks, and offer new behaviors than do dogs who have been physically corrected for making mistakes.

Prevention

Of course, it is not always possible to ignore a dog's inappropriate behavior. Some unwanted behaviors are self-rewarding, destructive, or unsafe, like barking at the mail carrier, chewing electrical cords or chasing cars. Management should be the first solution. It is easier to prevent unwanted behaviors than it is to correct them. It is far easier to keep your dog properly confined in a fenced yard or on a leash than it is to stop a dog with a strong prey drive from chasing cars, cats, joggers or skateboarders. While you manage the behavior, you also work to train a better level of control so the dog becomes more reliable around highly enticing stimuli.

NRM

Another approach is the use of a "No Reward Marker" or NRM. The NRM is a signal to let the dog know she made a mistake. It is not applied angrily, just used in a neutral tone to let the dog know that the behavior didn't earn a reward.

Commonly used NRMs include "Oops," "Try again," or the sound "Uh!" or "At!" A properly used NRM tells the dog that the behavior offered was not the behavior requested, and encourages the dog to try again.

Yet another positive behavior-correction method is to ask for (and reward) an incompatible behavior. A dog can't lie on her rug in the living room and bark at the visitor on the front porch at the same time. If we teach her that the doorbell is the cue to go lie down on her rug and stay there, she will no longer greet your guests with her sometimes unwelcome exuberance.

Positive Reinforcement

Anyone can use the basic principles used by scent dog trainers to obtain quicker, happier compliance from their own dogs. Keep these basic principles in mind:

■ *Love and respect are crucial. Your dog needs to know that you're on his side, not an adversary. "I had a dog in my last group that just would not open up to me," says USDA trainer Sandy Seward. "I spent probably the first week sitting in his kennel run with him. I had a Nylabone and he had a Nylabone, and we played Nylabone games. Once I got this dog to respect me and to relate to me, I found him to be more pliable in training."*

■ *Varying your rewards helps motivate your dog. If your dog never knows which fantastic reward to expect, he'll keep working his hardest. Give extra-special rewards ("jackpots") when the dog does something particularly outstanding, but occasionally throw in a jackpot for an average response. Other times, withhold rewards until you get an excellent performance. That way you always keep the dog guessing, and he's stimulated to work harder to get a greater reward.*

■ *Being afraid to move backward can often impede a trainer. Deciding to move forward with a lesson too quickly can stop a dog in his tracks. "A lot of times that's interpreted as the dog's inability to comprehend, but it's usually the trainer who has moved too quickly," Seward says. Step back and review previous lessons with a dog to make sure he fully understands and is comfortable with what you're asking.*

The Ongoing Debate

There is no lack of debate between trainers about the effectiveness of their various training approaches. Take the case of an aggressive dog. Compulsion trainers believe that such a dog must be physically corrected for the least sign of aggression: hackles raised, intense stare, growling. This teaches the dog that the behavior is not acceptable.

Positive reinforcement trainers suggest that a better approach is to change the way the dog thinks about the aggression-causing stimulus by associating it with positive things. If the dog's instinct is to get aggressive around children, for instance, the trainer might quickly give the dog a treat every time his canine student encounters children, so the dog will begin to associate the presence of children with "Good things happen," and the aggression will fade. Aggressive behavior is not lurking beneath the surface, because the dog no longer thinks of children as a threat; they are now a source of good things.

The arguments between the devotees of the various training camps will rage on forever. Clicker trainers tend to believe that force-based training dampens a dog's enthusiasm for learning, and "stifles their creativity." Compulsion trainers often express the view that reward-trained dogs won't perform reliably under stress. Clicker trainers say that violence begets violence, and that many dogs who are euthanized for biting were made worse by physical corrections. Compulsion trainers argue that their methods are faster, and that sometimes the use of force can cause quicker behavior changes that save a dog's life whose owner is at the breaking point and on the verge of sending the dog to the shelter.

Deciding on what training methods to use is up to the owners, but they can look to their dogs for help in making the choice. In the end, our dogs tell us the truth. We can find pet dogs and obedience show ring competitors from both training styles that are happy, reliable, willing workers, and we can find dogs from both training styles that are poorly trained and out of control.

However, there seem to be better results with the non-force-based methods. Much larger percentages of dogs in compulsion-based classes grudgingly comply with commands or look bored or disgruntled than in positive reinforcement classes, where enthusiasm usually abounds among all students in the class, two-legged and four-legged alike. And pet owners, left to their own devices, are more likely to follow their hearts and choose a gentle, non-violent training methods, while those owners who have been conditioned by past trainers and the pressure of competition to believe that a little "pop on the collar" won't hurt the dog, will more quickly accept force-based training.

Now let's go back to our imaginary stroll around the neighborhood. You're ready to sign up for a class, and just have to decide which one. Just put yourself in your dog's place for a moment and ask yourself which kind of class she'd prefer to go to. She'll give you the answer.

3

The Best Start

Starting off on the right foot is critical! Here's a primer on what you can accomplish during those important first few weeks.

Buddy was a tiny tan morsel nestled in his owner's arms, a perfect pudge of a yellow Labrador retriever puppy – eight weeks old, fat, round and chunky with a shiny black button nose, warm brown eyes and milk-sweet puppy breath. His owner, Tena, had carried him into training class to hand him over for three weeks of in-home boarding and training.

Generally, it's not recommended to send an eight-week-old puppy to a trainer for boarding and training. This is an important learning and bonding period for dog and owner; it is usually more beneficial for the two to learn together. But Buddy's owners had made some big mistakes in the two weeks they had owned their new puppy: First, they had purchased him at the age of six weeks, depriving him of a very important two-week period of education and socialization with his mother and littermates. Puppies taken away from their litters at this tender age often have problems with being mouthy (biting too hard on human skin) because they missed out on the chance to learn bite inhibition

from their mother and siblings. Unless they are given ample opportunity to socialize with other puppies or gentle adult dogs as they grow up, "only" puppies can become canine social nerds, failing to learn appropriate body language and other canine social skills. And sometimes, puppies taken away from their litters too soon grow up to be aggressive to other dogs.

The owners' second big mistake was adopting a six-week-old puppy two weeks before going on a three-week vacation. They had belatedly realized the folly of putting a very young pup in a commercial kennel for three weeks; hence, his three-week visit for bonding and training.

The day Buddy was dropped off, his owner gently placed him on the ground and he toddled along behind as we strolled down the driveway. Suddenly he stopped and sat in the middle of the road. We continued on, and when we had gone about 15 feet she turned back to him.

"What are you doing?"

"Going back to get him," she replied.

Big mistake number three—Buddy's owner was already getting "trained" to do what the puppy wanted!

"Leave him. He'll come."

We kept walking, Tena glancing nervously over her shoulder every three steps. Sure enough, we hadn't gone another 15 feet when Buddy jumped up and came galloping after us. The first lesson for Buddy (and for Tena!) was a success: We were the leaders, and it was his job to keep up with us.

Coming Home

"Home" had been prepared for Buddy's arrival. There was a plastic tarp in the living room covered with a thick layer of newspaper and a puppy pen set up on top of it. A variety of enticing chew toys awaited Buddy's needle-sharp baby teeth: A Kong stuffed with cream cheese, a bleached marrow bone filled with peanut butter, a Goodie Gripper with freeze-dried liver jammed into the holes, a Roll-A-Treat Ball full of tasty kibble, a couple of Vermont Chew Toys. We were ready!

This called for the "umbilical cord" approach to puppy management. Buddy would be kept at all times either in his pen, in the safely fenced and puppy-proofed yard with the other household dogs, on a leash or under direct supervision in the house. This would avoid a common mistake of novice puppy owners — giving the puppy too much freedom. The first few weeks of puppyhood are a critical time. If the pup's early behavior is well-managed, he will never learn to chew the furniture, climb on the counters, and urinate in the back bedroom. Through the judicious use of puppy pens, fenced yards, crates, adult dog baby-sitters, leashes and direct supervision, it is much easier to prevent unwanted behaviors than it is to unteach them.

Three Weeks With Buddy

The household's four resident dogs wouldn't hurt Buddy, nor would they tolerate obnoxious puppy behavior.

Buddy is taken inside and put in the pen, where he promptly begins to cry and shred the newspaper. This is where puppy owners often make another huge mistake. If his cries are heeded and owners relent, letting him out of the pen, he learns an important lesson—crying gets him what he wants. Instead, by being ignored, he learns that crying is not a useful behavior. I will teach him that crying is not a useful behavior. If a clicker is clicked ("Click!") and the owner produces a treat when he stops crying, he will learn to be quiet even faster. Buddy's cries, are ignored, and within 15 minutes he finally gives up and settles down for a nap.

Buddy's housetraining starts Day One, teaching him a verbal cue to go to the bathroom, and rewarding him for eliminating. At 11:00 p.m. he is awakened and taken outside on his leash. When he squats, he is told "Go pee!" When he is done, there's a "Click!" and a treat. After a short wait he also deposits feces, also accompanied by the "Go pee!," cue followed by a "Click!" and treat. This will happen every two hours throughout each day for the next three weeks, giving him lots of opportunities to do it right, and never giving him the chance to "make a mistake" in the house.

A common novice-owner error in housetraining is just putting the dog outside by himself, where he can eliminate anywhere he chooses. He might not even go to the bathroom at all, especially if he gets a treat when he comes back in. If "coming in" is the behavior that gets rewarded with a treat, he might as well skip the bathroom step!

Having other dogs to play with outside can also distract him from his bathroom purpose—he may be having so much fun playing that he forgets to stop and eliminate. But by having a person accompany him, he's taught to relieve himself a particular spot. (If he doesn't eliminate, he's brought back inside and returned to his crate for a while, then taken out to try again.)

Rewarding him immediately after he goes, ensures he knows why he is being rewarded. Using the "Click!" from a clicker gives him a clear message about which behavior is getting rewarded, even if the treat arrives a few seconds later. "Click!" will be used a lot with Buddy over the next few weeks. When he is done going to the bathroom, he's lead into the bedroom and a treat tossed into his crate.

"Go to bed," he is urged as he pokes his nose into the crate, looking for the treat. A gentle nudge to his tail pushes him into the crate, and he is ready for bed. (Within three days he will voluntarily go into his crate upon hearing the verbal cue, "Go to bed.") He has had a long, exciting day and is ready to sleep. He cries for a few minutes, but when he's ignored he curls up and sleeps through the night without a further peep.

The Routine

Housetraining

The following days fall into a routine that centers around Buddy. Wake-up—to a dry crate—is at 5:30 a.m., and he's rushed outside for his morning bathroom ritual, then back inside for breakfast in his puppy pen. The day consists of lots of trips in and out, interspersed with three meals, and several short training sessions. Within two days he is galloping into his pen at the "Go to your pen" cue, ready for his meal. He quickly learns to run up and sit for a Click! and a treat instead of jumping up on people. (This is accomplished in less than a day by ignoring the unwanted behavior—jumping up— and clicking and rewarding him with a treat when he sits.) By Day 4 he offers a sit for every possible occasion.

Release

He also learns to sit quietly in order to be released from his pen. When a person approaches the pen gate Buddy must sit in order to proceed. When he sits, the gate is opened. If he jumps up, the person turns away. Buddy quickly realizes that the sooner he sits and stays sitting, the sooner the gate opens. If he gets up before he is released, the gate is closed again. He doesn't even have to be asked to sit—he chooses to sit because that gets him what he wants—out! He is learning to control his own behavior without being nagged to do the "right" thing.

This is a key element of positive reinforcement training—teaching the dog to take responsibility for his own behavior rather than always being told what to do.

Down

On Day 3, after just one session with the clicker, he learns to lie down on a verbal cue. It starts by "luring" him down with a treat without even using the word "down," and "Click!" and treat when he does it. Once he does the "down" behavior smoothly, the word "Down!" is added to tell him what he is doing, as he does it, still clicking and treating for each "down."

After a dozen or so repetitions, the "down" is asked for first, then he is lured with the treat, followed by "Click!" and reward. It only takes a couple of dozen repetitions for Buddy to understand that the word "Down" means the same thing as luring "down" with the treat, and he is soon dropping like a rock to the floor on the verbal cue alone.

Bite

As expected, Buddy is excessively mouthy. When offered a treat, he chomps down on the hand that feeds him! His sharp little teeth hurt! Instead of punishing him for the pain he inflicts he is taught to soften his uninhibited bite. The treat is offered in a closed fist, and the discomfort of his teeth suffered until his bite begins to gentle. As soon as the bite softens, there are verbal cues: "Gentle," then "Click!," then, "Take it!" and the treat is given. He soon learns that he doesn't get the treat until he is gentle with his mouth. There is progress within a few days, but it takes the entire three weeks to get him as soft with his mouth as he should be.

A Constant Watchful Eye

Anytime Buddy is given house freedom he requires direct supervision. He wants to eat everything! Distracting him with the Chew Man only lasts as long as there is someone to play with him. There is work on increasing his self-control: He's asked to "Down," then "Click!" and a reward just for the down. Gradually the length of time between the cue for "Down" and the "Click!" and reward is increased. ("Gradually" means a few seconds at a time!) By the time Buddy returns to his owners, he will lie quietly at for as long as a half-hour.

He is walked on a leash to the mailbox every morning to get the newspaper, slowly overcoming his tendency to sit and wait to be picked up, and beginning to walk nicely alongside his human companion. He is "Clicked!" and rewarded a lot whenever he walks with his companion, but if he pulls on the leash it is a "stop and stand still." He soon learns that pulling does not get rewarded—the more he pulls, the longer it takes him to get where he wants to go.

Encouraging Good Behavior

On Day 4 the newspaper is lying on the ground. Buddy grabs it in his mouth. Having spent the last three days taking forbidden items away from him,the immediate instinct to take it out of his mouth must be stifled! This is a good behavior that we want to encourage! He carries the paper proudly back to the house, where it is traded for a treat. From that morning on, he fetches the newspaper every day.

It is possible to completely inhibit a dog's natural retrieving tendencies by punishing him every time he puts something in his mouth. However, Buddy is encouraged to pick up, play with and fetch *appropriate* play toys. the verbal cues you want him to learn are "Fetch" when he runs to get the thrown toy, and "Give" when he brings it back.

Of course, he doesn't know what "Give" means until it is taught to him. He is reluctant to unclamp his tiny jaws from his favorite chew toy, so a trade for a treat is offered. Bingo! He lets go of the toy when "Give" is said; "Click!" and a reward with a treat for good behavior follow. This same method is used to get him to give up a forbidden item, and thus avoid teaching him to play keep-away by chasing after him when he has something he shouldn't.

By the beginning of the second week there are new challenges for Buddy. He loves to splash in his water bowl, so he is taught to play in the water—in a baby's swimming pool. He is hesitant at first, but within a few days he is leaping into the pool to fetch his toys.

The third week is spent polishing his behaviors and preparing to return him to Tena. He has added "Come," "Stay," "Off," "Relax," and "Touch," to his repertoire. He sits and downs promptly on cue, and walks nicely on a leash. He goes into his pen and stays there without protest, sleeps through the night in his crate without a sound, and is allowed much more house freedom, although still with supervision. He can last six hours in his pen without soiling his papers, and in three weeks has only had one accident in the house.

Epilogue

It is exhausting! It takes so much work to properly raise a puppy! But there is an inherent satisfaction in shaping a puppy's behavior, watching him explore the world and teaching him to be a good canine citizen.

4

The First Command: "Come, Now"

Rewards, clarity and repetition are the keys to training your dog to come—every time you call.

"Come" is probably the most basic command every dog needs to learn. A dog that won't come when he's called is a danger to himself and others and a headache for his or her owner.

We've all been there: Standing hopelessly on the back steps calling and calling our dog, only to be ignored. Letting the dog off the leash to play and then discovering that part of the game is how long he can stay away from us.

There are techniques and principles that every owner, and their dogs, need to learn to master this basic command. The Dogwood Training Academy in Chamblee, GA is run by long-time dog trainer Nancy Patton. Nancy has been teaching all levels of obedience for all breeds since 1967. Nancy has ranked in the top ten in the United States Dog Obedience Championships since 1976 with golden retrievers, Shelties and Puliks, winning hundreds of awards.

Patton says the command "Come" is fundamental to all dog training. With this command you establish your authority, teach your dog respect for you and, of course, keep him out of harm's way.

But let's be realistic. Even though your dog needs to learn you're the authority figure, no dog will run to a human if he has experienced something unpleasant for his trouble. To get your dog to come to you every time, you have to make it worth his while.

"Come" needs to be the sweetest word your dog ever hears; it should always mean rewards, including praise. Never, ever call your dog to you to punish him, to give him a bath or for anything he doesn't like. "Come" must always mean that something good will happen to him, something far better than whatever he's doing at the time.

When you need to correct your dog, go to him; don't make him come to you. When it's time for a bath or a trip to the vet, don't call him to you; go and get him instead. "Come" should always be a word that means joy, love, hugs and treats, never punishment or unpleasantness.

First Step: Get Your Dog's Attention

Before you can start teaching your dog to come on command, you must first get his or her attention. Often this is more difficult than it sounds. Usually when you want your dog to come, he is into something else, usually involving sniffing. Until he learns, don't make the mistake of calling him when he is busy checking out something more interesting than you. A dog's name must be used only when you want his attention—never when you want to tell him off.. This holds true for his entire life.

If you have a puppy, it's a little easier; just rattle the pup's food dish. After the pup responds to that familiar sound a few times—meaning dinner time—start saying "Come," followed by his new name and he will soon start to respond and associate all three cues; eating, "come," and his name. When you're sure he recognizes his name, find a time he is roaming aimlessly looking for something to do then call him. If he responds, you're off to a successful start in getting his attention.

The human voice is a very effective tool when training a dog. Learn to cultivate yours. Try not to sound angry when you are delighted with him. The actual words you use mean nothing—the tone is all important. Even if you're angry, use your normal calling voice. Otherwise he'll know he's in trouble and the old "fight or flight" response will kick in.

Later on when you are training him to walk properly on the lead you can use his name to get his attention. Granted, keeping his attention is an entirely different matter. Small puppies cannot pay attention to anything for very long, so be prepared to accept just a few seconds at first.

As he grows older he will be able to concentrate for longer and longer periods. But learn how he reacts and don't try to make him pay attention for a second longer than his limit. Err on the side of caution.

Come!

Your dog understands English about as much as he understands Greek or Swahili. Dogs respond to cues. In the case of an oral command, when he responds he's reacting to a memorable sound.

As with all dog training skills, find one command for the desired action and stick with it. Obviously, if you want your dog to come, the word come is a natural. The hard "K" sound is easy for the dog to hear and understand. If you prefer "here," or any other word, then by all means use it.

Be consistent. If you yell "Come here boy," one time, and "Here, boy," the next, it can be confusing for the dog. He needs to filter out the command part and if he's confused he won't respond correctly. Extra words are superfluous; your pet only understands the "come" part, and if it is mixed in with other sounds he may miss the command entirely.

Treats And Tricks

Food, carefully used, is a great motivator for dogs, especially pups. But make him earn his tidbits. Some people think that it is good enough just to throw food at a dog. It isn't. It must have a meaning for the dog or it is wasted.

Toys are also good; especially if your dog isn't motivated by treats, or if you're worried about your dog's "waistline." Have a special toy that the dog likes and keep it only for training sessions. Produce the toy and ask him to watch. If he gives you his full attention for a second or two, break off and play. Try for another second the next time and gradually build up. Don't ever be so predictable that your dog knows exactly what you are going to do next. That will just teach him to keep only half his attention on you. If his eyes are on you he is concentrating. If not you are wasting your time.

Play with him as much as you can. Let him learn that his time with you is the best thing that could happen to him and he will start to give you his complete attention. In essence, you'll become his ultimate toy.

But he also needs to know when you're serious. Serious doesn't mean threatening; otherwise, you'll see a "fight or flight" reaction. Only when you have that level of understanding can any serious training begin.

Who's In Charge

Dogs understand pecking order. You're the boss, and the sooner your dog learns that in your relationship the better. Give him an inch and he'll run all over the yard. Repetition is the key. You yell "come," the dog should come.

Patton recommends working with the dog every day. You can start with a short lead attached to his collar. Separate yourself from him by a few feet and say "Come." When he comes, give him a treat and praise him. If he doesn't come, give him a tug until he does. Then don't scold him, give him a treat and praise. Once you're sure he understands, give him more slack in the lead and do it again. Then more slack. Do not allow detours enroute. Once you're sure he fully understands (and can be trusted), let him off the lead and call him from a few feet away.

Throughout the day, stop what you're doing for a minute and call your dog. Reward him handsomely when he comes. It doesn't matter if he's three feet away, or in a different part of the house. Call him and reward him when he comes. Practice often and make coming when called the most enjoyable thing in your dog's life.

Be patient. Don't expect your dog to get it right away. Most trainers believe you shouldn't feel confident that your dog will come immediately, every time, under any circumstances and in any place until you have repeated the command at least tens of thousands of times. Even then, remember, training only increases the probability of a correct response; there is no perfection. When a dog makes a mistake, try to be positive in your response. Treat it as a benefit to the training process, an additional opportunity for communication between you and your pet.

DOGS UNDERSTAND PECKING ORDER. YOU'RE THE BOSS, AND THE SOONER YOUR DOG LEARNS THAT IN YOUR RELATIONSHIP THE BETTER.

Praise

Up to this point we've encouraged, in essence, rewarding your dog. He comes when called and you give him a treat. This raises the possibility of him making a connection between the stimulus ("Come") and the response ("Coming"). Ultimately, praise should be enough; so once you're sure he fully understands and comes every time, wean him off the treats. After all, he's supposed to do what he's told, right? Still, people always feel the need to quit using food for training long before they should. Eventually you'll need to: you don't always have food to give, but your praise will always be there.

It takes a good deal longer to train effectively than most people think, so don't be in a hurry to drop the treats until you're sure it is no longer necessary.

Lying Down On The Job

As you know from playing with your dog, he has boundless energy. That energy also means he can probably outlast you. If you haven't taught the dog properly to come, he just might lie down. He knows that eventually you'll just go away.

If your dog knows you'll yell "Come" three times before you come after him, he'll wait for the third time (or five or six) before he'll respond. Why? Because that's the way you taught him. If you want him to come the first time he's called, teach him that. Start when you're working with him on the lead. Call once, if he doesn't come, give him a tug.

If you know your dog understands the command to come but does not respond to you when you call, don't waste time calling his name over and over. He'll just keep on ignoring you. In the process, he'll learn that it's okay to ignore you.

Instead, go get your leash. Call him again using a happy, encouraging voice but only give the command once, no more. He heard you the first time. If he doesn't respond, go and get him. When you catch up with him, don't scold or punish him. Just snap his leash on and go straight to the house. No punishment—but no rewards either.

Scolding

Sometimes a dog needs to be punished. Since not all dogs are the same, there are those who need a firmer hand. Since words themselves are irrelevant, let your tone of voice do the scolding.

Remember though, don't expect him to come to you so you can scold him. You'll need to go to him. Don't worry that your dog won't like you. If a dog is treated with love, the love in return is practically unconditional. In fact, Patton says, the more the dog respects you, the more intense the bond between you and your dog.

Playing And Training By Tugging

From tiny Pomeranians to huge Mastiffs, dogs love to play Tug o' War. There is an inherent canine joy in growling, grabbing, pulling, shaking, ripping and shredding that satisfies a dog's basic predatory instincts. Owners also find it rewarding to roughhouse with their four-footed friends, and a Tug 'o War game is a great way to take the edge off a high-energy pooch.

Many trainers caution against playing Tug 'o War with canine companions, warning that it teaches a dog to be dominant and aggressive. However, if you play the game right, it's a perfect opportunity to teach your dog deference and good manners and you can even resolve aggression problems. Only if it is done improperly does "Tug" teach your dog bad habits.

The first key to playing the game right is that you always win. At least almost always. At least in the beginning. The Tug Toy is a very special, cherished object. It is kept hidden in a special place, and only comes out when you want to play. Tease Woofie with the toy—shake it a squeak it, and use a word such as "tug" or "pull," that you chose for your behavior cue. Let your dog grab one end, and have a great time tugging and shaking the toy with him for a few minutes, then offer a very tasty treat.

If you've used a sufficiently tasty treat, your dog will open his mouth for it. When he does you say "Drop," or "Give," since he must drop the tug toy to eat the treat. You just won the game. "Click!" a clicker or tell him "Yes!" to let him know he did a rewardable behavior, then hold the treat and let him nibble it while you safely remove the tug toy. Now you can either play again (playing the game again is another reward for giving up the toy when you asked) or put it away and play again later.

Before long, your dog will be programmed to drop the toy on cue, and you can win whenever you want. Now you can let him grab it and run off with it every once in a while to make the game more interesting. Just remember to have him give it back to you when his turn is up—don't start playing chase!

Some dogs want to play too aggressively with a tug toy, and some dogs get seriously aggressive. If Rambo plays too rough, and either jumps up on you or puts his mouth on your clothing or skin, it's time for an instant "time out!" Just say "Too bad!" in an upbeat, cheerful, non-punitive tone of voice and put the toy away for a few minutes. If his rowdy behavior persists, use a tie-down, a crate, a puppy pen, or just step out of the room briefly. After a moment or two, resume the game. Every time he bites or gets out of control, it's "Too bad!" and a time-out. Four time outs in a row ends the game for the day. Rambo will learn very quickly that when he is too rough, playtime is over. Very soon he will begin to control his behavior so that he can continue playing the game.

5

Click!

It may sound—and be—farfetched, but here's how training chickens can teach you to more effectively train dogs.

Training chickens? What an odd idea! Yet all across the country, animal owners and trainers are flocking to workshops put on by a legendary husband-and-wife team, learning how to train chickens...so that they may better train their dogs. Here's an account of one such workshop, held recently in Monterey, California.

In The Presence Of Legends

At 9 a.m., on a cool, cloudy morning in late September twenty-two dog trainers, from all over California (and one from Illinois), were perched on the edges of their chairs, waiting with nervous anticipation for the workshop to begin. Bob and Marian Bailey, legendary animal trainers, had towed their little yellow trailer and 16 educated chickens all the way from Hot Springs, Arkansas to Monterey, California, and were now poised at the front of the room, ready to begin the two-day workshop that would unveil the finer points of clicker training to the group.

Training chickens, the Baileys had promised, would allow us to hone our skills on a species of animal that was especially food-focused, and that reacted with lightning speed. This would improve our timing and sharpen our powers of observation, so that we could then go home and apply our newly learned skills to training dogs

— or virtually any other species of animal. We could learn from our mistakes with the Baileys' chickens without jeopardizing our own dogs' training programs.

THE CLICK! SOUND SERVES AS A MARKER SIGNAL, OR BRIDGE, THAT GIVES THE ANIMAL INSTANT FEEDBACK ABOUT WHAT BEHAVIOR IS DESIRED.

A Positive Click

Clicker training is an informal term used by many trainers to mean "applied operant conditioning," that is, **training with positive reinforcement**, wherein the clicker trainer uses treats to reward the animal for a desired behavior.

The Click! sound serves as a **marker signal**, or **bridge**, that gives the animal instant feedback about what behavior is desired. The animal quickly learns to figure out what behavior produced the treat, and to reproduce that behavior for additional treats.

This method of training is easy for the average dog owner to use, because it does not require a lot of practice and skill; it only requires an open mind.

Marian and her first husband, Keller Breland, were the first trainers to use **operant conditioning** for practical applications, back in the 1940s. The couple founded Animal Behavior Enterprises (ABE) in 1943, and proved that the then-new scientific principles of operant conditioning developed by B.F. Skinner could be used to train virtually any kind of animal, exclusively by reward, without punishment.

The Brelands worked with Skinner during World War II, training pigeons to guide missiles. They also created training programs and manuals for dolphin trainers—methods still in use today at attractions like Marine World and Sea World.

During this phase the couple began working with Bob Bailey, who, in 1964, was the first person to make a successful release and recovery at sea of a trained dolphin. Following Breland's death in 1965,

Marie and Bob continued to work together, and eventually married.

All told, over the past 55 years, the three trainers have trained more than 140 different species of animals using Skinner's principles of operant conditioning and the techniques they developed and applied over the years.

After Karen Pryor introduced clicker training to the dog training world in 1984 through her exceptional book, *Don't Shoot The Dog*, the demand by dog trainers and owners for the Bailey's knowledge increased exponentially. Their two-day chicken workshops grew in popularity, as did their five-day Chicken Camps, held at their expansive training facility in Hot Springs.

Prerequisites Of Good Trainers

Bob immediately put the class at ease with his comfortable manner, easy charm, and sense of humor. He opened with a discussion of what it takes to be a good trainer—quick reflexes, strong powers of observation, and an understanding of the species you are working with, as well as the eccentricities of the individual animal.

Bailey got down to the nuts and bolts of chicken wrangling with the first hands-on exercise, designed to teach participants the finer points of chickenship: how to pick one up (quickly), hold it (wings pinned to prevent flapping), and carry it around (tucked under the arm).

The first several exercises involved learning the mechanics of delivering the Click! and food reward to the chicken in a precise and timely manner when they demonstrated the behavior we wanted. In the first exercise, the goal was to reward the chicken for pecking a target, to begin with, a large black circle.

"One peck only!" Bob reminded us again and again. "Get the food there faster! Avoid falling into a rhythm or the chicken will learn the rhythm rather than the behavior! Don't let your body language telegraph your intentions to your chicken!"

The students practiced the mechanics of Click! and reward with varying degrees of coordination and success. Some were adept and followed Bob's instructions to the letter. Some immediately fell into a rhythmic pattern of reward delivery despite Bob's and their partner's reminders.

Dog owners face similar challenges when marking and rewarding their dogs in a training class.There is an art to knowing how to time the click! and to reward the "trainees" properly, and trainers need to teach owners how to do it, rather than just assume they already know the proper timing.

Grab Your Chicken!

Some participants were quite comfortable handling their chickens, while others were decidedly intimidated. Bob's suggestion that the more confidently you handled your bird, the less likely you were to get pecked, seemed to do little to ease fears. Only the constant repetition of chicken-handling exercises convinced the less-confident handlers that they could safely handle the birds. Bob also talked about what to do if your chicken got loose on the floor. ("Don't everybody chase it! Offer the food cup.")

And if you spilled your food cup on the table in front of your bird? "If something goes wrong," Bob advised, "grab your chicken."

These observations, of course, have applications to dog training, where there are also wide variations in confidence levels with dog owners in training classes. Perhaps incorporating similar handling exercises the first week of class could increase some owners' levels of confidence and competence with their dogs. Certainly it is true that if your dog gets loose, chasing it only encourages it to run away from you — just like the chickens.

And just as the workshop chickens were attracted to the food cups, so, too, are dogs that have been trained with positive reinforcement attracted to the reward cues — the rustling of a plastic bag, or a Click! for an instant of rewardable behavior, such as a pause or a glance over the shoulder as the errant dog moves away from you.

Principles of Operant Conditioning

While the chickens rested in between exercises, Marian Bailey took center stage, teaching proper training vocabulary and lecturing on the principles of operant conditioning. A **stimulus**, she reminded, is any change to the environment to which an animal can respond or react. **Reinforcement** means strengthening a response to a stimulus. **Extinction** is the weakening of a response to a stimulus through non-reinforcement.

When we train through positive reinforcement, we reinforce behaviors by marking (clicking) the ones we want, and extinguish the behaviors we don't want by ignoring them (non-reinforcement) rather than punishing them.

For example, a dog that tries to get attention or food by barking will quickly learn that barking is counterproductive if you turn your back when the barking starts. If you are consistent in your response, the barking will eventually extinguish. He will learn this lesson even more quickly if you Click! and reward him as soon as he is quiet, and gradually extend the length of time you expect him to stay quiet before clicking and rewarding. Most owners inadvertently do the exact opposite, by ignoring the dog when he is quiet and paying attention—"shushing" the dog—when he barks, thus teaching the dog that barking gets him the attention he craves.

ABCs of Behavior

■ ***Antecedents*** *are events that occur before the behavior. We can increase the dog's response to the antecedent if we make it more salient — that is, we make it stand out from the other stimuli that are present in the environment by giving it meaning. A cue, or signal, for a dog to do something is given meaning when we show him that the appropriate response to the cue will be reinforced (with a treat).*

■ ***Behavior*** *means anything that the dog does, such as sit, lie down, come, bark, jump up, run away, eat, dig, howl. A response is the particular piece of behavior we have selected to work with.*

■ ***Consequences*** *are events that happen after a behavior or response takes place.*

For example, if your dog sits when you say "Sit!," you give him a piece of hot dog. The word "Sit!" is the ***antecedent****, the dog's sit is the* ***behavior****, or response, and the piece of hot dog is the* ***consequence****.*
The kind of training you have employed is called ***operant conditioning*** *because the dog's response (sit) operates in the environment — that is, it has an effect on, and at least to some degree, controls the consequence.*

Training Concepts

Over the course of the two days, the class taught the chickens increasingly complex behaviors. While at first they were rewarded for pecking at a large target, they progressed to a small black circle, and then to a tiny red dot from a laser beam. We discovered that a chicken can be taught to distinguish between several different-colored but similarly shaped pieces of paper and to peck the correct one. (This is called discrimination. An example of its use in dog training is the scent discrimination exercise in Utility obedience classes where a dog must select the article with his owner's scent on it from among a number of other times that are identical in appearance.)

We also taught our birds to pick up and stretch a rubber band (we held one end, they pulled on the other), and then did "chaining," which means teaching the animal to perform a series of behaviors. We taught our chickens a simple two-behavior chain — to stretch the rubber band and then peck a target before getting the Click! and reward.

While we trained the chickens, we were learning important concepts for dog training: **The timing of the reinforcement is critical.** You must know and visualize exactly what kinds of behaviors you will Click! and reward, or you will be late. When your reinforcement is late, you are actually rewarding the wrong behavior.

For instance, if you are trying to teach your Chihuahua to retrieve, you might begin by clicking and rewarding him for touching his nose to a ball. You must Click! the instant his nose touches the ball, and follow the click with a treat. If you are late with the Click! you will be reinforcing him for moving away from the ball rather than for touching it. While an occasional late Click! is not critical, routinely clicking too late can prevent Bowser from learning to fetch the ball.

It is also important, we learned, to **break down a complex behavior into tiny increments**, making sure the animal thoroughly grasps each step before proceeding to the next. According to the Baileys, the biggest mistake most trainers make is trying to go too fast.

For example, when your dog suddenly seems to lose the concept of the behavior you are trying to train, it is a sign that you may have

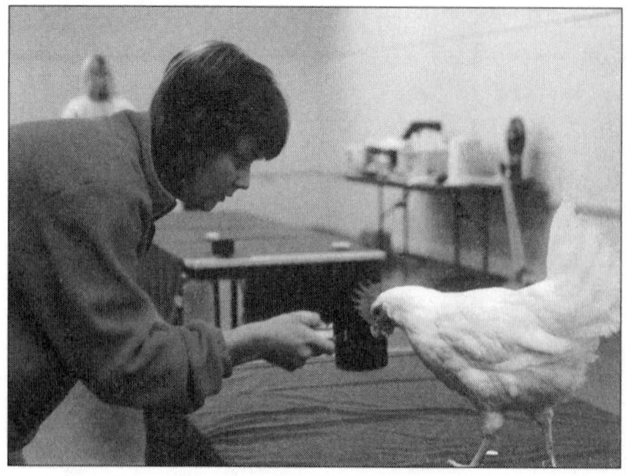

A student gives a chicken its reward. Chickens are quick and food-oriented, making them perfect partners for teaching people about training.

Left, the chicken is put through an exercise in discrimination. Presented with three identical shapes of varying colors, it quickly learns to peck at the correct color to receive a food reward. Right, chickens (and dogs!) can be taught to perform virtually any behavior that is physically possible for them. Here, the chicken is taught to pull and stretch a rubber band to get its treat.

taken too big a step forward. Step back to the last place the dog was doing well, reinforce the behavior there, and figure out how to break the next step down into smaller increments.

Slow, Steady Progress

Let's say you have succeeded in getting your Chihuahua to reliably pick up the ball on cue. In your excitement over your success, you now toss the ball across the yard and give the dog the cue to pick it up. The Chihuahua, not being a natural retriever, stands and looks at you uncomprehendingly. You have taken too big a step.

If the dog has been picking up the ball from the ground directly in front of him, go back and repeat and reinforce this response a few times. Now you might try moving the ball just a foot away and giving the cue. If that is too much, you might try six inches, or three, until he gets it, and then continue increasing the distance in small increments, until he will fetch the ball from across the yard.

In order to avoid making the mistake of going too fast, according to Bob, you should analyze the topography, or shape, of the behavior before you begin to train a new behavior. Then you should create a written training plan, and lay out the goals for each session. While you may have a goal in mind for each session, you must also be flexible and be prepared to revise the plan if it isn't working, by re-analyzing the behavior and looking for different ways to approach the training, perhaps breaking down the steps into even smaller increments.

Clicker Training: Fun, Fast, Flexible

Clicker training, communicates the "good dog" message quickly and clearly when your dog does what you want.

Making Noise: *Clicker training allows you to mark desired behavior exactly when your dog performs it. Most people use a plastic-and-metal thumb clicker, but any noisemaker (such as a standard ballpoint pen) that can make a consistently audible sound will do. "The marker should be a novel but consistent sound that your dog can distinguish from more familiar sounds in its environment—including your voice," explains Karen Pryor, a behavioral biologist and author of Don't Shoot the Dog, a book on positive reinforcement.*

Click 'n Treat: *Once you've got a suitable noisemaker, click the clicker precisely when your dog does something you like and follow up quickly with a tantalizing food treat so the dog associates the sound with yummy reinforcement. Treats should be small but potent—a savory morsel your dog adores rather than its regular kibble or run-of-the-mill dog biscuit. The timing of the click in relation to the desired behavior is crucial. "If more than a half-second elapses between the behavior and the click, you will inadvertently reward behavior that happens after the behavior you want," notes Dr. Gerry Flannigan, a resident at the Behavior Clinic at Tufts University School of Veterinary Medicine.*

Target Practice: *Once your dog understands the basic click-and-treat scenario, introduce a target stick (a dowel or yardstick) as the foundation for eliciting specific behaviors. Hold the target stick in front of your dog and click as soon as the dog touches the stick with its nose—which most dogs do naturally out of curiosity.*

Steps to Success: *Break "big picture" behavior into smaller tasks. Once your dog has a small behavior down pat, such as touching the target stick with its nose, use that success as the springboard for training a different but related behavior, such as touching the stick with a paw..*

Vocal Cues: *When your dog reliably performs a certain behavior, add a vocal cue such as "high five," then click and treat only behavior that obeys that vocal cue. Never correct, reprimand, or punish a dog that doesn't heed the cue. Simply don't click and treat. "The opposite of reward is not punishment; it's no reward," explains Dr. Flannigan.*

Piquing Interest: *To teach a new behavior, you have to click and treat every time it occurs. But once your dog knows the behavior, click and treat only intermittently and randomly. "Sporadic rewards keep the dog enthusiastic about playing 'the game,'" explains Dr. Flannigan.*

Who's Training Whom? *One of the beauties of clicker training is that it engages the dog's mind. In fact, "clicker training is about getting the dog to think, 'What can I do to get this person to click?'" says Ms. Pryor. "It's not a rigid technique, and it's fun for both people and dogs."*

Reinforce, Reinforce!

A key concept is giving lots of reinforcement. Many dog owners and trainers are too stingy with the Click! and reward. If you don't give enough reinforcement, you lose your dog's attention. Our chickens were quick to hit the floor and look for stray bits of food if the rewards were coming too slowly up on the table.

Our dogs also are easily distracted in the very stimulating environment of a dog training class if we don't give them a good reason — plenty of Clicks! and treats — to stay focused on us.

Students also tend to stop giving rewards too soon. My dogs, although they are well-trained and will respond without food rewards, still gets lots of reinforcement— praise, petting and treats.

Responding to my requests for behavior is their job, so I make sure I "pay" them for doing it. Most people wouldn't continue working unless they got paid. Why should our dogs work for free? 🐾

6

Training Beyond The Basics

Training can be more than just endless drills. New methods and goals provide fun for dogs and owners alike.

Not so very long ago, trainers assumed that anyone who signed up for a basic obedience class was seeking that perfectly straight, sit-in-perfect-heel position. Classes were conducted with military precision, trainers barking commands as owners marched their dogs in a circle, jerking and popping on leashes and choke chains in order to achieve lightning-fast responses. Success was measured by speed and perfection of position, and advanced work was conducted with one goal — to show in American Kennel Club obedience competitions, earn obedience degrees, and achieve scores as close to that magic "perfect 200" as possible.

A New Training Paradigm

My, how the times have changed! A relatively few years ago, many trainers began to realize that the greater percentage of dog owners in their classes really only wanted a well-behaved companion—a trustworthy family dog. Who cared if the dog was sitting three degrees off perfect? Most owners were just happy the dog sat at all, and couldn't have cared less about scores in the obedience ring. Thus began a paradigm shift in the dog training world, from obedience competition training to family dog training. With that shift has come an exciting vista of advanced training opportunities and breathtakingly fun dog-related activities.

Untapped Skills

All of our dogs are capable of doing far more than we ask of them. Their senses, especially hearing and olfactory, are so highly developed that they can perform feats that appear miraculous. Their physical abilities are awesome, as demonstrated by the prowess of highly-skilled Frisbee and Agility dogs. And they have talents that reveal the versatility and breadth of their potential to think, reason and learn—if only we tap into it.

Today, there are more possibilities for canine recreational activities than ever. Mixed breed dogs, once second-class citizens in training classes, can now compete in obedience through the American Mixed Breed Obedience Registry (AMBOR) or the Mixed Breed Dog Club, and at national obedience competitions. They can also join their blue-blooded brothers and sisters in agility, herding, flyball, Frisbee, tracking, drill team, square dancing, musical freestyle, My Dog Can Do That, Canine Good Citizen Tests, animal assisted therapy programs, K9 games, tricks classes, lure coursing, (take a breath) television, advertising, movie work, water dog sports...There is something out there for every dog's talents.

IF YOU HAVEN'T DISCOVERED YOUR DOG'S HIDDEN TALENTS, PERHAPS YOU'RE NOT LOOKING, OR YOU NEED TO CULTIVATE HIS CREATIVITY

Developing Your Dog's Potential

Dogs who are encouraged to engage in activities that stimulate them mentally and draw upon their inborn talents are less frustrated and better behaved than their less fortunate littermates who languish, bored and lonely, in their backyards. Owners whose dogs are less frustrated and better behaved can appreciate their dogs more, enjoy engaging in activities with them, and are more likely to fulfill their social contract to provide a lifelong loving home for their canine companions. The new, non-competition-based classes that rely primarily on the use of positive training methods are the best approach to developing a dog with acceptable social skills while building an unbreakable bond between canine and human.

Discover the talent!

If you haven't discovered your dog's hidden talents, perhaps you're not looking, or you need to cultivate his creativity. Here's how you can encourage your dog to develop his full potential for amazing behaviors:

■ Spend more time with your dog. In order to uncover your dog's hidden talents you have to have a relationship with him. Dogs who live in the back yard 24 hours a day may have all kinds of talents, but you will never know. The more time you spend with your dog, the more likely you are to notice his astounding abilities.

■ Encourage spontaneous behaviors. If you are on the lookout for talent, you are more likely to spot it when it occurs. If you have conditioned your dog to a reward marker (the Click! of a clicker or a verbal "Yes!" that tells your dog a treat is coming), you can mark and reward him when he does something cute, useful or creative that you would like him to repeat. You will be surprised how quickly your dog can learn to deliberately offer behaviors that you capture with a Click!

■ Consider your dog's genes. Scent hounds are bred to follow their noses. Chances are good that your beagle or Basset Hound's hidden talents might lie in the tracking field. Golden retrievers, Labradors, and the herding breeds tend to have a natural aptitude for retrieving, thanks to decades of genetic selection for bringing back waterfowl, game birds and sheep.

If you know what your dog was bred for, you know where to start looking for talent. Don't limit yourself to the genetic predisposition, however—plenty of dogs' talents lie far afield of their genetically selected behaviors.

■ Provide learning opportunities. The more you expose your dog to different environments and new stimuli, the more likely you are to discover his hidden talents.

■ Set your dog up to succeed. Manage his environment so he can experiment and explore without getting into trouble. The more he is punished for trying new things, the more he is likely to shut down and stick with tried and true behaviors that he knows are safe. We want him to offer new behaviors so we can reward them.

For instance, if we want to encourage retrieving, we must make sure we don't leave shoes, books, and kids' toys where he can get them, then yell at him for picking them up. The more often we punish him for putting his mouth on inappropriate items, the more likely we are to destroy his interest in retrieving. The more we reward him for picking things up, the more we reinforce the retrieving behavior.

Of course, not all hidden talents are useful. Some, such as opening the refrigerator and snitching the chicken, can be annoying or, worse, dangerous. While we may admire Rover's ingenuity, we also need to stop him from hurting himself or destroying valuable possessions. In cases like this it is often easier to prevent or manage the behavior than to retrain it. It is simpler to install a latch on the refrigerator door than to set up complicated booby traps to extinguish a behavior that Rover has found exceptionally rewarding. Restricting access by closing doors, putting valuables in a safe place, or using crates, pens or leashes, can go a long way toward extinguishing unwanted talents without stifling canine creativity.

Basic Training—The Foundation

Basic training is the foundation for any of the more advanced canine activities. If you are interested in pursuing the less formal doggie activities, you can start by finding a basic class whose trainer is more interested in making sure her students — both two-legged and four — have a good time while they learn than maintaining strict discipline in the canine classroom. Once you have graduated from a basic training class you are ready to explore the big wide world of more advanced canine activities. Here are several of the many activities now available in most parts of the country. See *Contacts & Resources* for more information.

My Dog Can Do That

A board game you play with your dog — whoever heard of such a thing? These days, more and more dog owners have, as word spreads about *My Dog Can Do That (MDCDT)*. This delightful game requires the use of positive reinforcement training methods. Owners pick cards from any one of three decks, at three different levels of difficulty. Each card describes a "trick" or behavior that the dog has to do. Examples of each level of difficulty are:

■ Beginner: Dog sits still while player skips ten feet away and stops.
■ Intermediate: Dog lays down, rolls over, then stand up.
■ Advanced: Dog retrieves a toy and drops it in a basket five feet from the player.

Owners can use treats, praise, hand signals, and other verbal or body language cues as needed, but no anger or force; no pushing, pulling, jerking, or yelling. You can play it as a family game, with each member of the family taking turns drawing a card and working with the dog. You and your dog can play against your friends and their dogs. Or you can take part in the increasing number of MDCDT matches and tournaments that are being held around the country.

Be forewarned — dog owners who are serious about this game have already purchased it and are practicing all of the behaviors on the cards with their dogs in preparation for competition. You'd better hurry if you want to catch up! Animal shelters and training clubs are starting to offer MDCDT competitions as fund raisers.

Agility

It's an obstacle course for dogs, complete with tunnels, jumps, a teeter-totter, and several other items to challenge your dog's agility. Dogs of all shapes and sizes love it — experienced dogs run an entire course by themselves while the owner stands in the middle of the ring. Three of the four organizations that sponsor competitions welcome mixed breed participation, so there's no excuse — anyone can play!

Flyball

You have to see this one to believe it. Flyball is a hurdle relay race for a team of four dogs of any heritage. Each dog in turn jumps four jumps, spaced ten feet apart. At the end of the jumps is a flyball box. When the dog touches the pedal on the front of the box a tennis ball shoots out. The dog catches the ball and goes back over the four jumps to the owner waiting at the starting line. Then the next dog goes. The team that finishes first wins. Flyball is a very competitive sport, and great fun to watch. Dogs with an affinity for retrieving tennis balls adore this game.

Herding

When you think of sheep or cattle dogs, you tend to visualize Australian Shepherds and Border Collies. But the list of dogs that can be taught to herd includes multi-purpose breeds with herding ancestors way back in their bloodlines, and mixed-breed dogs with some herding blood. And the list of breeds that are officially designated as herding dogs is much longer than most people think — some 30 breeds, including the Rottweiler, Tibetan Terrier and the Samoyed. Multi-purpose dogs that can herd includes another dozen or so, including such unlikely breeds as the Kerry Blue Terrier, Poodle, Soft-Coated Wheaten Terrier, and Schipperke.

Herding is the perfect outlet for the high-energy Border Collie and the other intense herding breeds, as it makes full use of their extreme intelligence and obsessive herding behaviors.

Musical Freestyle

Affectionately known as "Dancing With Dogs," Musical Freestyle (AKA Canine Freestyle) the newest doggie sport is most akin to a combination of ballroom dancing and pairs figure skating. People and dogs dance together to music of the person's choosing, in a routine choreographed to complement the dog's personality and abilities The routine can range from short and simple, to long and complex.

Animal Assisted Therapy

Therapy dogs can be any breed, mix, size shape or color, as long as they are well-behaved, can tolerate disturbing events like rolling wheelchairs, falling crutches, and patients who don't always behave like other people, and who enjoy being the center of attention.

There are national organizations that provide certification for therapy dogs, and many local humane societies offer therapy programs. These programs always welcome new volunteers because the demand for animal-assisted therapy is so high.

Imagine how it would feel to be deprived, long-term — maybe forever — of the touch of your dog's soft fur, or the caress of her warm tongue.The human handlers speak of miracles — of non-responsive patients who move, even speak for the first time in months when a therapy dog greets them; of faces that light up when a furry friend arrives.

Frisbee

We've all watched them in awe — on beaches, in parks, and during half-time at football games — those incredibly athletic dogs that leap eight feet off the ground and catch a Frisbee in mid-air. Frisbee is an activity you don't even have to go to a class for — all you need is a dog who loves to jump and retrieve, and, of course, a Frisbee. Even dogs who aren't naturals at it can learn to play Frisbee, and there are loads of resources — books, information available from Frisbee Clubs, and Internet web sites. For those who like to get serious, there are Frisbee competitions almost everywhere, up to and including national canine Frisbee championships. Be sure to have your veterinarian OK your dog's participation in this activity.

Tracking

A tracking dog follows the scent trail left by a human being (or other animal) that has passed along a particular route. Tracking can be done as a hobby (for fun), as a sport (to earn titles), as part of a serious effort to save human and animal lives through Search and Rescue work, and in law enforcement as police K9 units track criminal suspects. The ability of a dog to follow scent trails that are "invisible" to the human nose seems uncanny, but we all know that a canine nose is thousands of times more sensitive than a human nose.

Section II

Four Trainers

7

Pat Miller

Nonviolent, non-force training methods preserve the trust and relationship between dog and handler.

Pat Miller consistently comes up with positive, effective methods for teaching dogs to desist their undesirable behavior—as well as with fun methods for teaching them entertaining and useful behaviors. She is passionate about the importance of using only nonviolent, non-force training methods, which, she ably demonstrates, compromise nothing in terms of effectiveness, and preserve the trust and relationship between dog and handler.

You are a very compassionate and firm advocate for animals. How did your opposition to force-based training arise?

Pat Miller: It didn't exactly happen overnight. Over the 20 years I worked at the Marin Humane Society, I increasingly developed my personal philosophy of respect for all life. It made less and less sense to me that we constantly jerk around these animals that we are supposed to respect.

But the epiphany happened when I was training my dog Josie for Utility. I had already taught her to retrieve for competition in the Open class, and although we were successful at that level, it took a technique known as the "ear pinch" to teach her to do it. The ear pinch is a common method to train a retriever in traditional training circles. You pinch the dog's ear over the choke chain to cause her pain; when she opens her mouth to protest, you put the dumbbell in her mouth and release the pinch on the ear. This teaches her that in order to make the pain go away, she needs to pick up the dumbbell. Josie had always loved training, and was always very willing to work with me, even when I subjected her to the hurt and indignity of having her ear pinched.

However, when we moved up to the Utility level of obedience competition, I had to teach her to retrieve metal dumbbells for the scent discrimination exercise—and Josie *hated* the metal articles. She did fine with the leather dumbbells, but she refused to retrieve the metal articles. My trainer kept telling me to pinch harder, to force her to do it. But finally one day I got out her scent discrimination articles to get ready for a training session and Josie disappeared. I found her hiding under the deck and she wouldn't come out. It still brings tears to my eyes when I think about it. She was telling me in the only way she knew how that she just couldn't do it, and I finally realized that I had to stop trying to force her to do it. I just wouldn't do that anymore.

For a while, I literally stopped training my dogs. They were all well-versed in basic house manners, but I stopped training for competition altogether.

What prompted your return to training?

PM: There were several concurrent events that led me back, about seven years ago. I started hearing about this new, positive way to train, one that didn't involve the use of force. I started reading about it and decided it was something that I wanted to do. I first read Karen Pryor's book, *Don't Shoot the Dog*, and later, Jean Donaldson's book, *The Culture Clash*. These books really confirmed and supported my thoughts that the way most of us think about and treat dogs is so wrong-headed. *Don't Shoot the Dog* was my introduction to clicker training—the powerful and logical use of positive reinforcement in training. *The Culture Clash* explains how to understand what's going on in your dog's brain, and debunks the Lassie and Rin Tin Tin myths about how dogs exist only to please us. Donaldson emphasizes that dogs do what works for them; they don't have an intrinsic desire to please us, but they do learn that by pleasing us they can often get what they want. Of course, they sometimes learn they can also get what they want in ways that don't please us. We can understand them better, get along with them better, and accept them better for who they really are when we understand how to positively motivate them to do what we want.

Around the same time I was reading these books, we got a new trainer at the Marin Humane Society, Trish King. Trish was a member of the Association of Pet Dog Trainers (APDT) and was interested in positive training, and she helped with my evolving training

Pat Miller, with "friends." Miller is a proponent of non-force, non-violent training, methods which are grounded in positive training techniques.

philosophy. Then I joined APDT, and that really advanced my development as a positive trainer. Probably the best source of my ongoing education has been the APDT email list, which you can join if you are a member of APDT. It's a forum where trainers from all over the world can network and share training ideas and questions. If I encounter a dog with a problem that I can't find a positive solution for, I can go on that list and receive all kinds of suggestions.

After using and teaching positive training methods for a few years, do you think there is any place in dog training for force-based training methods or punishment?

PM: Well, punishment can work. Certainly, hundreds of thousands of dogs have been turned into well-mannered, amiable companions and top-notch canine competitors as a result of punishment-based training methods. But, because of the potential for serious negative repercussions of punishment, many dogs have been ruined as a result as well. There was a time when dogs who didn't respond well to punishment were viewed as untrainable, incorrigible, impossibly defiant or unworkably soft. Many of those dogs were euthanized, often after they bit someone in their desperate attempts to protect themselves from violence. Today we know better.

With positive, gentle training methods, most dogs who aggressively resist force-based training can be motivated to willingly and happily respond to our cues. Because we don't use force, we don't trigger the escalating cycle of violence that too often leads to physical harm to dog or handler. The "soft" dog who was unable to tolerate the physicality of compulsion training blossoms under reward-based training. And the dog with a stable personality who was able to respond to punishment-based training can also perform at least as well, if not better, in the hands of a positive trainer. We are just beginning to see the new generation of positively-trained dogs winning titles and awards in the canine sports arenas. And more and more dog owners are realizing the wonderful difference in the quality of the relationship they have with their gently trained dogs.

Some individuals in the traditional dog training community have a number of lingering prejudices against certain positive methods—the use of food as a lure or as a reward, for example. What is your take on the use of food in training?
Food is a powerful motivator; it's one of the essential things a dog must have to live. Why wouldn't you use such a powerful tool to motivate a dog to do what you ask him to? Food facilitates what has been called the "Helen Keller moment"— that magic moment when suddently, the student "gets it"—with dogs better than anything else. Once the dog understands that his "good deeds" make good things, such as tasty treats, happen, he is invariably willing and eager to produce innumerable good deeds! In essence, he learns that he can make you give him treats by being a "good" dog.

In a long-term training program that employs positive reinforcement, once the dog understands the basic premise—good behaviors make good things happen—you can eventually move away from constantly using food as a reward to using other, what we call "life rewards," such as chasing a tennis ball, chasing a squirrel, swimming, going outside, coming inside, being petted, being praised. I do recommend using food rewards at least some of the time to keep the dog's enthusiasm level high, but some dogs will be more enthusiastic about performing in exchange for a game of fetch than for a treat.

But I hear arguments from people all the time about using food…
PM: Well, some people think that dogs should do things for us just because they love us, or because they recognize our inherent "mastery." I have heard the trainers say that the dog shouldn't feel as if it has a choice to obey or not. Training with force and punishment only motivates the dog to do things to avoid the punishment, but they still have a choice—and you can see them choosing not to perform in the competition ring all the time! If dogs never chose to do

the so-called "wrong thing," you would commonly see perfect scores of 200 in the obedience competition—but you don't! I would rather my dog chose to do the "right thing" because it is frequently rewarding, rather than choosing not to do the wrong thing because she knows she will be punished.

I wouldn't be training professionally today if I had to do it the old way. Not only is positive training gentler and more respectful of the dog—another living being—but also, it works, it works beautifully. It might take you longer to get your dog to lie down for the first time using positive methods than it would if you just jerked her feet out from under her with a choke chain, but positive trainers are convinced that a dog trained using positive methods learns the behavior *reliably* more quickly.

I used your methods with a young puppy for a photo shoot recently and was able to get the pup to lie down for me within seconds by luring him with a treat. I can't believe how fast it works...especially once the handler "gets" it! Do you find that people sometimes need more help than dogs in your classes?
PM: Trainers have a saying that the dogs are easy, it's the people who are a challenge. It's a common mistake for a trainer to train a dog to do all kinds of things and then hand it back to the person who can't make the dog do anything. Obviously, this makes the owner feel inadequate and angry. Yes, I actually do more people training in my classes, because once the person gets it, the dog is generally easy.

Do you use positive reinforcement for your human students?
PM: Of course! I give out what I call "bonus bones," slips of paper that they can redeem at graduation for prizes. I give them out any time the student does well—asks a good question, answers a question well, does an exercise correctly, rewards their dog appropriately. At the end of each night of class, the person with the most bonus bones wins a prize. It's fun, and it demonstrates to them how well positive reinforcement keeps a pupil motivated.

Miller has a lifelong relationship with dogs; she was the child in her family, she says, "who was always teaching the dog to shake hands and jump over a broomstick in the living room."

She began her professional career as a horse trainer. In 1976 shebegan volunteer work at the Marin Humane Society in Marin County, California where she spent 20 years, the final 10 as Director of Operations. Concurrent with this work she apprenticed for four years with a top obedience trainer and competitor.

In 1996, Pat began Peaceable Paws, her own training business in Monterey County, California, before following her husband, Paul Miller, to Chattanooga, Tennessee, where he is the director of that city's animal services program. Pat opened a new training facility in Chattanooga, and is finishing a book about positive training methods. She also Chairs the Ethics Committee of the Association of Pet Dog Trainers.

8

Dr. Ian Dunbar

How to teach any dog when and how to bark, and when and how to stop, using reward-based training methods.

Using three simple methods, noted trainer Dr. Ian Dunbar teaches us how to train any dog *when* and *how* to bark, and *when* and *how* to stop barking. Any one, or all three methods can be used.

Start with the simple understanding that dogs bark to communicate. If that is our underlying premise, the idea of dealing with a "problem barker" becomes a whole lot easier. It changes our focus from doing anything we can to make the dog "shut up" to figuring out what the dog is trying to say—so we can address his concerns, and thus find more constructive and quieter ways for communication to occur.

When helping owners with problem barkers, my immediate goal is to calm the dog and teach it to bark less, regardless of why the dog is barking excessively. It's not important to me as a trainer to know why the dog is barking. However, if I even suspect that the dog is stressed or in pain, first I will calm and quiet the dog and then I will address its underlying problems. Some dogs may have very good reasons for barking, and I strongly encourage owners to investigate these. I especially encourage owners to use TTouch and other handling and gentling methods to check to see whether the dog is sore or hurting in some way, and because these methods are most relaxing and enjoyable for dog and owner.

I'm going to offer **three methods** to alleviate your dog's problem barking and to teach your dog to bark—and stop barking—on command. The first is **simple management**. The second is **reward training**. The third is a fun method—**lure/reward training**. Use any one method, or all three.

Thoughtful Management

The first thing I recommend—and I recommend this for all dog owners, whether or not their dogs bark—is that the dog be fed out of chew toys. This method works especially well for owners who are at work all day. Stuff the dog's usual meal into six different chew toys and when you leave in the morning, put them in different locations all over the house. Better yet, tie several different chew toys full of food in the dog's crate (with the door open) or fasten them to an eyehook in the baseboard next to the dog's bed. To get his dinner, the dog has to go to his resting place and play with his chew toy.

It's a simple fact that a dog cannot sniff and chew and bark at the same time. You reduce his opportunities to bark by giving him something constructive to do for a good part of his day. This is especially effective because each piece of kibble rewards the dog for not barking!

Within three days to one week of feeding your dog his daily meal in installments or several courses, stuffed into chew toys, you will have a completely and utterly different dog. I guarantee the dog will not only be barking less (and you can measure this while you're gone with a sound-activated tape recorder) but also, he will be calmer, will have learned to settle down and enjoy quiet moments on his own, and have little inclination to become a destructive chewer.

Reward Training

Ironically, humans are the major cause of excessive barking in dogs. Most owners inadvertently train their dogs to bark, by *ignoring* the dog when it is quiet, and especially, by *responding* to it when it barks. Dogs quickly learn they can get their owners to react if they just make noise. By getting off the couch and saying, "Oh, Rover, please, hush now," or even by yelling "Shut up!" you are doing just what the dog wanted you to do: paying attention to him. The dog thinks, "Gosh, this barking thing works great! I just got him to wake up!" Dogs also learn to bark to get their owners to pet them, to open doors for them, and even to serve them supper!

Conversely, if you only pay attention (i.e. reward the dog) when he is quiet and specifically when he stops barking, and you simply ignore him when he barks, you will quickly shorten the barking sessions. Of course, you can also reward appropriate barking. When the raccoons are breaking into the cat's food on the back porch, or a stranger is standing on your front porch, you want the dog to bark. But a few barks will do it; it doesn't require 500 barks.

Murphy's Law of learning: If you put a behavior problem on cue, it becomes an obedient response, says Dunbar.

Say you want the dog to bark when someone is at the door, but you also want the dog to quiet down quickly after the doorbell rings. Recruit a friend to help you with a training session. Ask him to ring your doorbell every couple of minutes.

The first time the doorbell rings, and your dog explodes, go to the dog, and say, "Good boy," and then wait for him to stop. If you really have a problem barker, this might take a few minutes—even as many as 20 minutes. He might go crazy, barking, sniffing, huffing and puffing. It doesn't matter how long it takes; make sure your friend has a chair to sit in and a book to read out there on the porch. Eventually the dog will stop.

When the dog stops, and stays quiet for at least three seconds, say effusively, "Good boy Rover! Cookie? Here's a cookie for a Shush dog! Here's a Shush cookie. Good Shush cookie." (I suggest using the dog's normal dinner rations in these training sessions, since you can go through a lot of food doing this.)

Then, during the next couple of minutes, while the dog is lying with you quietly, say to him, "You're a good Shush dog. Would you like another Shush cookie?" and give the dog some more kibble.

At about this time, when your friend has heard nothing but silence for a few minutes, he should ring the bell again. The dog will undoubtedly go nuts again. Say, "There's a good dog, Rover," gratefully and politely, but not enthusiastically. Wait until he stops barking to turn on the charm. "Oh good dog! Good Shush dog, Rover! Want a Shush cookie? Good dog!"

Building On Success

After you've gone through this about 10 times, you can prompt the dog to start slowing down his barking while he's still in the middle of it. "Ding-dong, ding-dong" "Woof woof woof woof" "Thank you, good dog, Rover."

Then, after about 10-15 seconds of barking, say, "Good dog, Rover. Would you like a Shush cookie? Good dog!" By this time, the dog will have learned that he has to be quiet to get the kibble. Wait for at least three seconds of silence before you give him the treat. If he starts to bark again, ask him again, "Do you want a Shush cookie?" and hold the treat where he can see it. Count to yourself, "Shush cookie one, Shush cookie two, Shush cookie three," and if he still hasn't barked, you can give it to him.

The dog is learning two things. The first is, "Barking is OK, my owner actually kind of likes it, especially when the doorbell rings, but he likes it better when I'm quiet" Second, he's learning that it's a really great thing to stop barking when you say Shush.

From the time of this session on, keep a jar of kibble at the front door. I would certainly expect the dog to bark more if a real guest comes, but now you can have the guest come in, and you can say, "Thank you, Rover. Now Shush!" Eventually the dog will stop barking, if only to sniff the person. At that point, you say, "Good Shush!" and you give the dog a cookie.

I like reward training; it's very calming. This is because you don't give any commands; you just wait...the desired behavior will eventually come.

Whatever your dog's problem may be, I'll bet you're convinced he does it all the time. You say he barks all the time. Look! He's not barking now! You say he runs off in the park and won't come back. Well, it might take him a long time, but he does eventually come back, right? If you were to highlight these moments, they would quickly become the best moments of the dog's life, and he would strive to do them more often.

Lure/Reward Training

Owners who have a really good connection with their dogs and who like training can use the lure/reward method to train their dogs when and when not to bark.

Before I describe this method, however, I want you to acknowledge that barking is a normal dog behavior. It would be inhumane to stop them from barking completely.

Also recognize the optimum time for training. It is not a good time to train your dog to Shush when the UPS guy is at the door, or it's 2 a.m. and there are possums all over your backyard. The deck is stacked against you at times like that.

Train your dog to Shush when you and your dog are relaxed, following a bit of TTouch, for instance, or a cup of tea or meditation! That's a great time.

...REWARD TRAINING IS VERY CALMING. THIS IS BECAUSE YOU DON'T GIVE ANY COMMANDS; YOU JUST WAIT...THE DESIRED BEHAVIOR WILL EVENTUALLY COME.

The only problem is, the dog is relaxed, he's not barking. That's why we train the dog to bark on cue! Does this sound dumb? I call it "Murphy's Law of Learning": If you put a behavior problem on cue, it becomes an obedient response! But the other reason to put the behavior on cue, is so that we can decide when to train the dog to shush. We'll do it as a training exercise, and not out of necessity at a totally inappropriate time with lots of distractions.

To train the dog to bark on command, we use the old "Request—Response—Reward" sequence. We say, "Speak!;" the dog goes, "Woof woof;" we say, "Good dog!," and give him some kibble. Only now, to speed up the training, we are going to lure the dog to bark in a "Request—Lure—Response—Reward" sequence, with you indoors with your dog and your friend back with his book on the front porch.

Suddenly, you exclaim with urgency, "Rover! Speak! Speak! Speak!"—the request. Hearing this, your friend rings the doorbell—the lure. Instantaneously, the dog barks—the response. You praise the dog for barking, "Good dog, Rover!"—the reward. And then, after five to seven seconds of barking, you say, "Good dog Rover, now Shush," and you hold a piece of kibble right in front of his nose. As soon as he sniffs the kibble, he'll stop barking; these are mutually exclusive behaviors. Praise him as he sniffs. "Good Shush one, good

Shush two, good dog Shush three," and give him the kibble.

Repeat this half a dozen times and, if dogs thought like we do, they would muse, "Hmmm. How do these owners always know when the doorbell is going to ring?" But what dogs actually figure out is that you always says, "Speak!" just before the doorbell rings. "Heck, I'm just going to bark when he says, "Speak!' I'm not going to wait for the doorbell!" That's the first stage of lure/reward learning. The dog has learned that the request always precedes the lure which causes the response, at which point the lure is no longer necessary.

In other words, by about the tenth try, when we say, "Rover! Speak! Speak! Speak!," the dog will erupt into action—and our friend, hearing this, will know he doesn't have to press the doorbell this time.

After this one session, your dog will know Speak and Shush, and you'll no longer need the doorbell—though you will owe your friend a nice lunch.

...A DOG CANNOT SNIFF AND CHEW AND BARK AT THE SAME TIME.

Advanced Training

Now you can teach the dog at which stimuli you would like it to bark, at which stimuli it must bark, at which stimuli you would prefer it not to bark, and at which stimuli it must never bark.

For example, I had a dog once who wanted to bark at every person walking down the sidewalk in front of my house—not an acceptable activity in a quiet neighborhood. However, I do want my dogs to let me know when a person walks into my yard or is coming to my door. So I planned a party one morning, and I deliberately told all of my guests to arrive at different times. I also instructed them to walk up and down the sidewalk six or seven times before walking up the path that leads to my front door. Then I sat with my dog by a window that overlooked the sidewalk and path.

The dog barked at the first person who walked by, and I said, "Shush, Shush, Shush," and did my best to quiet her by holding kibble where she could see it. By the time my friend walked down the sidewalk four times, the dog had become more interested in her kibble, which she sniffed and received as a Shush reward. The next three walk-bys were quiet, and I rewarded my dog with much praise and more bits of kibble.

Then my friend entered my front path. As his foot struck the first step on the path, I exploded, saying, "Speak! Speak! Speak!" as if there was some kind of amazing emergency. Startled, the dog let forth a barrage of barking, and I praised her as my friend walked up the path and came in.

With the help of my friends, by the end of the morning, I had produced a dog who, to this day, enjoys nothing more than sitting and watching the front sidewalk, just dying for someone to step onto the property so she can let loose with barking. I had taken a problem behavior and created the best burglar alarm that money can buy, and best yet, I can sleep with it! 🐾

Dr. Ian Dunbar is a veterinarian, animal behaviorist, and writer. He received his veterinary degree and a Special Honours degree in physiology from the Royal College (London) and a doctorate in animal behavior from the University of California at Berkeley. Dr. Dunbar has written 4 books and 17 booklets on dog training, and has produced 11 training videos (see Appendix). Dunbar is also the founder of Sirius Puppy Training (in 1971), and the Association of Pet Dog Trainers (in 1993). His latest venture is the PuppyDog AllStars K9 Games, a showcase in California.

9

Sabra Learned

How to establish more quiet and effective lines of communication with our dogs using TTouch.

Using Tellington TTouch, Sabra Learned believes we can learn how to hear what our dogs are saying and establish quieter and more mutually beneficial ways to communicate with them. Here, she addresses the problem barker.

Dogs bark for a reason. Always. Yes, really. Even the non-stop barking of your neighbor's dog (it's never OUR dog, right?) is "for a reason." Dogs bark to communicate—with us, with other dogs, with the squirrel next door.

When your dog barks to let you know there's a prowler outside, or there's smoke coming from the oven, or that a strange dog is outside and your toddler is on the lawn, we're grateful for the message. There are times you want your dog to bark; it's just a question of when and how you want them to do it and which methods you're going to use to teach them what you want.

Then there's the dog who barks, sometimes incessantly, for no apparent reason, and we're definitely not grateful for the message. Tellington TTouch recognizes that problem barkers also have a valid message. By paying attention to it, we have the opportunity to engage in a dialogue with our dogs and work cooperatively to establish quieter and more mutually rewarding ways to communicate.

The content of a problem barker's message may be emotional: ("I'm home alone and I feel abandoned!" "We've moved and I'm confused!" "No one has ever trained me and I don't know what else to do!" Or physical: "My back hurts!" "I'm freezing out here!" "I'm old and can't hear well, so I'm barking at everything just in case!" Or mental, reflecting what's on the dog's mind: "Sirens!" "Strangers!" "I'm bored and that squirrel is driving me nuts!"

Few of us agree that these kinds of messages should be conveyed through an endless volley of barking. But by acknowledging that the message exists, we can change our perception of it from "He's doing it on purpose to drive me crazy!" to "How can I help him express himself more constructively and quietly?"

TTOUCH HELPS RELEASE THE STRESS AND TENSION THAT IS BEING HELD IN THE DOG'S BODY...

Detective Work

Tellington TTouch gives us two ways to address the problem barker: Via his environment and problem solving, and via his body and our hands. The first part is mainly an information-gathering process. By observing when and how the dog barks, where his focus is, and what's going on around him, with him, and to him, we have a chance to clarify some of the triggers that are setting him off.

Sometimes you have to be a veritable Sherlock Holmes to detect and solve the problem. One client whose dog seemed to bark totally haphazardly did extensive research, studying her dog's environment: the garbage schedule, the mailman's route, traffic patterns, smells...and still couldn't figure it out.

I happened to come on a windy day, and heard a neighbor's wind chimes while waiting at the door. During my questioning, I asked if there was any correlation between the chimes and the dog's barking and Voila! Her light bulbs went on, the wind chimes came down, and the problem was solved.

Giving the dog lots of praise for barking when you want him to (i.e. a stranger in the backyard) and a short acknowledgment when it's something inconsequential ("Yes, I see the person walking by. Thank you for telling me.") you'll give the dog a clearer picture of the information you would like.

There are other easy solutions. If the dog barks at people going by, put up curtains or close the blinds so the dog can't look out that window. If the tone of your doorbell sets your dog off, use a knocker. The more you define, support, and acknowledge their role in the house the less they'll feel a need to create their own.

TTouch

The second way to help problem barkers is to apply the techniques of TTouch (see to help them regain their physical, emotional, and mental balance and help them learn better, more effective strategies for coping.

TTouch works directly on the nervous system, using specific circles, body movements, and learning exercises in a non-habitual way to stimulate body awareness and activate new neural pathways to the brain. Sounds good, but what does it mean?

TTouch is education for the body and mind. By bringing awareness to the body, fear and tension can be recognized and released, old negative patterns can be examined and discarded, and new information can be evaluated and accepted. The benefits include increased self confidence and self-control, and improved health and behavior.

TTouch practitioner Sabra Learned strokes the dog's muzzle, stimulating the limbic center in the brain, the seat for emotions and learning. This "mouth work" is one way to help an animal release fear and tension.

That's why TTouch is especially helpful for dogs who bark mindlessly—the ones that just don't know how to stop. That kind of frantic behavior creates so much stress and tension in the body that they then can't think anymore, so that any little thing that makes them bark automatically rolls over into obsessive or compulsive barking.

TTouch helps release the stress and tension that is being held in the dog's body, which both makes the dog more comfortable and rational, and reduces his arousal level—that is, reduces his immediate physical response to stimuli, so that instead of habitually reacting, they are able to think. This helps them to make better, more mutually beneficial choices.

Any kind or amount of TTouch will help a compulsive barker, but some of the exercises—what we call the "mouth work"—are especially appropriate. Barking is an oral occupation, and so by working with the mouth, you help bring the dog's attention to it. For example, a TTeam practitioner might slide their hands across the dog's muzzle, massage and gently stretch the lips, and tap on the tongue and the roof of the mouth.

Another huge benefit of TTouch is it can be learned relatively easily. The deeper connection it brings between you and your dog—the increase in trust and respect you will receive from listening to and honoring their message—is a priceless gift and a beginning well worth pursuing. 🐾

Sabra Learned, of Berkeley, California, has more than 30 years of experience working with animals in a variety of holistic healing modalitiies, and has also extensively studied the patterns and expressions of animal learning. She found an expression for both areas of interest in her work as a TTouch practitioner. Learned teaches TTouch to animal caretakers in private and group lessons and workshops. She also is a frequent volunteer in her local animal shelters, where she takes a special interest in helping abused or stressed dogs regain their health and emotional wellbeing prior to adoption.

10

Vicki Hearne

Reflections on communications among dogs and humans, and how training can resolve dog problems of every kind.

Vicki Hearne is a nationally known dog trainer, poet, and philosopher who has written widely about animal behavior and training, and believes that dogs possess language, individuality, and a moral sense. She and her husband train dogs out of their home in Connecticut.

Tell us about your new book.
Vicki Hearne: I'm working on a project called *First Friend*, which is about a number of notions I have on my mind. The secret subtitle is "The Cultures of the Dog." Dogs, like people, have tremendous talents and affinities for—and antipathies to—certain kinds of landscapes and terrains, both literal and cultural. For example, I'm a terrier person. I find that terriers are deep. But now I also have a border collie. And there was a real culture clash between my terriers and the collie until they figured out how to communicate with one another.

That's interesting, because we always think that dogs all have the same language, no matter what breed they are.
VH: Oh, no. There are more dog dialects than there are dog breeds.

We've read training books based on the premise that bitches teach their puppies how to communicate with other dogs, so that they understand other dog's signals. The premise is that you can build a training program based on the mother dog's teaching methods.

But some dogs appear not to have been taught anything by their mothers.
VH: Well, there are some good mothers and some who aren't. Labradors, for example, are so mellow, even with their own offspring, that often they don't teach good manners with other dogs. A friend of mine has Labs, and she sometimes borrows one of my Airedale bitches to correct her puppies. I own four Airedales. One of them came my way as a result of a hard court case. He's from a long line of Southern hunting dogs. In a hunting trial, you have to keep him on a leash or else he will take apart the Hav-A-Heart trap to get at and dispatch the raccoon.

The other three Airedales are from efficiency lines, and they're the ones who make a good point of making sure their puppies have good manners. Other dogs teach other things. For example, many dams will teach their pups footwork and body English. They teach their puppies that they don't get to run around in the house, but only outdoors. It is the mother who begins housebreaking.

There's been a lot in the media recently about the use of psychotropic drugs, including antianxiety drugs like Prozac, to control unwanted animal behavior. What is your opinion about the use of drugs to control animal behavior?
VH: I'm holding back judgment. There is a deep ethical divide among dog trainers and behaviorists about using a correction to interrupt a behavior. One side says, "Go for drugs because they are nonviolent." The other side says, "How nonviolent is it to invade the brain?" Trainers often don't like to use them because sometimes the dog is too drugged to learn. But I want to see a little more in the way of hard clinical evidence that these drugs affect dogs' brains the way people say they do. I would like to see autopsies being done on dogs, a lot of autopsies, especially now that dogs are being diagnosed with conditions like autism.

Clomicalm has been approved by the FDA to treat separation anxiety. Is that a condition you have treated?
VH: I have never failed to cure separation anxiety without drugs. Dogs are den animals. In my experience, the dog who is allowed to walk about all day long, in and out of the house with the kids and so forth, but gets no training, is still a bundle of nerves. If you take the same dog, crate him, go through a separation anxiety program, and work your dog for 20 minutes to an hour a day, he'll be much happier than the dog who is just rattling around the landscape. Dogs need work to do. If they have that to look forward to, they go into a

Robert Tregesser

kind of suspended animation in the crate. As long as a dog trusts his owner, he's content to be in that crate. In many respects, trust matters a lot more to dogs than love. For some dogs, love may not matter at all.

Do you think that many behavior problems can be resolved by a good training program?
VH: In California, where you can give training classes year-round, I would give a ten-week class. The last week of class would be graduation, and a judge would come and give a CD [Companion Dog] test. At the beginning of the ten weeks, you would find that most people were there because of a problem they were having with their dogs. Well, problem night wouldn't be until week six. So I would ask about the problems, and I'd say seventy percent of them would look around at each other. They'd be scratching their heads, saying, 'You know, he really hasn't done that for a while.'

At the end of *Adam's Task*, you wrote that you would be interested in working towards Companion Dog legislation that would grant well-trained dogs the same rights as guide dogs for the blind. Did anything come of that?
VH: Just in the past few months a group of us have formed a sort of mini-list on the Internet called the North American All-Girls Trainers Association. These are all women who know perfectly well that not only can you train a dog so that you can walk down the street off-lead, but that you can do it on St. Patrick's Day during the parade in New York City.

How would you go about demonstrating that level of control to skeptics—of which there are many?
VH: You would arrange for a regular obedience trial, with all the levels—Companion Dog, Utility Dog, and so forth-and add on one extra class. You would have the handler drive up a car, about 50 to 100 yards from the opening of the ring. Between the ring and the car would be a corridor of distractions. A nice hot bowl of tripe, a pony and a goat if you could get them, teenagers with blasting radios, a raccoon on a lead, and anything else you could think of. The judge says, "Open your door," and the dog must wait with no commands

until the judge says, "Call your dog." Then you would heel forward through the corridor of distractions. When you get there, the dog and handler perform a normal CD test by either AKC or UKC rules. If the rules are UKC, the dog will have to jump a hurdle on the recall and will at another time do an honor down while one other dog works in the ring.

After the individual exercises are completed, there will be group stays, off lead, with the handler out of sight. Sit stays would be required only if the rules were UKC, because the dog has already done an honor down with the handler out of sight. If it's AKC rules, you would have both long sits and long downs with the handler out of sight.

Whether the rules are AKC or UKC, the recall will be at least a hundred yards long, and he must go back through the corridor of distractions while a dozen or so handlers are wandering back and forth over the dog's path. The dog must negotiate all this without becoming distracted or confused. Then he waits again, until the command is given to get back in the car.

Aren't there pretty specific laws banning dogs—except for guide dogs for the blind—from most places?

VH: There are no federal laws about where dogs can and cannot be. There are lots of Department of Health regulations in municipalities. But you could take this on at a very local level. You could take on your own neighborhood. You take the videotape of the obedience trial to the town council and make the point that these people have put in so much work to get their dogs to that level of control. You point out that trained dogs make cops feel safer. Dogs, even small ones, are a much better deterrent to rape than even martial arts or weapons. The kind of idiots who are thinking about an attack figure they can fake out a human being, but they don't have that confidence about faking out a dog. So they are liable not to make the approach in the first place.

Do you think there is support for this kind of Companion Dog law among places of business?

VH: I think plenty of business people would be glad to allow dogs in, but if they let some dogs in and not others, they will anger their customers. So you ask the town council to say that businesses maynot/must-allow Companion Dogs on to the premises. We could start bringing the dogs out of exile. It will take awhile. You'll walk into a restaurant, and there will be a Saint Bernard under the table. People will do a double-take. But this is already done in other places.

They do it in France. Anything they do in France we ought to be able to do.

Do you think it would catch on with owners who aren't otherwise interested in obedience training?
VH: I think the idea of what a genuine, trained dog can do will seep into the public's consciousness. One well-trained dog will cause the people who let their hellions run loose to become ashamed. And when people observe a dog behaving so beautifully, they will want their dogs to be like that. People don't realize how much their dogs are capable of. When they see working obedient dogs, their response is often, I want that, too. I want that relationship with a dog.

Vicki Hearne's 1986 book, Adam's Task: Calling Animals by Name, *discussed the special relationship between people and domesticated animals, especially dogs and horses. In it, Hearne argues that dogs possess language, individuality, and a moral sense.* Bandit: Dossier of a Dangerous Dog, *published in 1991, recounted Hearne's efforts to save a remarkable dog sentenced to death for biting. The case, widely publicized at the time, revolved around the furor over the almost universal perception of "pit bulls" as an inherently dangerous breed. Hearne also published a collection of essays in 1993 titled* Animal Happiness. *She is the author of three volumes of poetry, and one novel about dog trainers,* The White German Shepherd.

Section III

Problem-Specific Training

11

Teaching Social Skills to Difficult Dogs

Impending aggression: How to recognize it, how to head it off—before it becomes an out-of-control problem

Dogs fight other dogs for many reasons. They fight in aggressive play. They squabble over food and toys. They challenge each other for the best spot in the pack or the best spot on the bed. They fight to protect their puppies and other canine pack members, or to defend territory and their humans. Some fight because they've been bred or taught to fight. And a surprising number of dogs fight just because they are poorly socialized; they've never learned to speak "dog," and as canine social "nerds" they inadvertently display body language that triggers aggressive responses from other dogs. Serious dog-on-dog aggression is a common problem, and one that is often overlooked and too often tolerated. However, it is not normal dog behavior, and, in many cases, it can be prevented or mitigated.

All dogs are capable of turning on one of their canine acquaintances with a short but ferocious attack. If this happens only occasionally, these brief (though dramatic) interchanges are actually normal – a device dogs use to set boundaries regarding what kind of behavior they won't tolerate, or to establish dominance over each other. But dogs that frequently attack other dogs without regard to the victim's behavior can cause owners a lot of trouble, heartache, and even lawsuits.

A tiny percentage of these canine bullies are born, not made; certain breeds were developed to fight each other. But far more dog-aggressive dogs are made that way by their owners—through a lack of proper socialization, inappropriate human intervention in normal canine interactions, even encouragement of aggressive behavior. In other cases, a dog slowly develops increasingly aggressive behavior that goes unchecked or unnoticed by his owner—at least until it gets bad enough that the dog seriously injures someone else's dog.

It's very frustrating for social, responsible dog owners when they end up with a dog who can't get along with other dogs. Understandably, few people want to walk with them. The walks they do take are fraught with tension, as they try to control their dog and warn other owners to keep their distance. Eventually, many people tire of the stress, and dominant canine bullies end up exiled to back yards, or even put to death.

Regaining Access

Fortunately, with appropriate training, many of these social misfits can regain access to society. Some trainers occasionally offer special classes for such dogs—"Growl" or "Difficult Dog" classes. These are designed to teach owners new skills for dealing with their dogs' antisocial behaviors.

One goal of the class is teaching owners how to detect and interpret their dogs' aggressive body language in time to avert confrontations with other dogs. They learn exercises that can distract their dogs from their habitual and aggressive focus. The owners also learn to use food lures, rewards and praise to reinforce desired behaviors.

The other major goal is to give the dogs opportunities for learning appropriate dog social behavior from each other. In the wild, dominant body language is most frequently used to avoid fights, since it is contrary to pack survival for dogs to go around routinely injuring each other. Most dominance moves are bluffs, designed to intimidate the opponent into bloodless submission. Occasionally, a brief scuffle ensues, rarely causing serious injury. Thus dominance in wild packs is usually settled and maintained with relative non-violence.

Owners of domestic dogs tend to be phobic of any display of aggression between dogs. Because of the perceived risk of serious injury to the participants, owners don't let dogs "fight it out" in an uncontrolled setting, so most dogs never experience the natural consequences of their aggressive behavior. Therefore, minor, normal, usually harmless, scuffles are often treated as major crises. The dogs are yanked apart and punished mightily. As a result, not only do the dogs not learn how to settle their squabbles peacefully, their levels of stress and aggression actually escalate and they become more aggressive around other dogs. It becomes, literally, a vicious cycle.

In a Growl Class, dogs can be allowed to interact to the point of learning those consequences—with an important difference: they wear soft but strong muzzles. In this controlled setting, dogs safely get past their initial burst of aggression so they can get to the part where they learn to relate appropriately.

It's critical that dogs and owners enrolled in these classes be pre-evaluated by the trainer. Classes are then custom designed to meet the needs of the students. Protections are put in place so that big bullies are prevented from trouncing the timid dog who bites in self-defense. Where appropriate, owners can be shown some of the exercises ahead of time so their dogs get extra practice. A bully might need to spend more time practicing his "Off" exercise, while a very nervous dog might get extra homework assignments in "Relaxation Techniques."

By the end of the course, some dogs can be fully integrated into their local canine community. Others can be given supervised freedom in a designated "play group." Still others will never be trustworthy for off-leash play, but will be under much better control and far safer on-leash than previously.

The best results will be enjoyed by highly motivated owners who enjoy close bonds with their dogs. Dogs who are responsive and connected to their owners and who are easily motivated by food, praise, or other rewards are most likely to benefit from this type of class. Independent dogs who are oblivious to their owners' presence and behavior requests are more likely to fail.

Muzzles for Safety

For safety, some aggressive dogs should wear a muzzle. The best muzzles are soft but strong. These are comfortable for the dog, can be fitted snugly behind the dog's head, and allow enough freedom to eat treats. Muzzles should not be worn for more than 15-20 minutes, since they restrict the dog's ability to pant and self-cool.

Typical Class

The mix of people and dog personalities (and mixed results) displayed in a recent Growl Classes is fairly typical. Four dogs were selected to participate: Beau, an eight-year-old neutered male Rottweiler mix; Kito, a three-year-old neutered male Akita; Jessie, a four-year-old spayed female Australian Cattle Dog mix, and Schmaal, an eight-year-old spayed female Saluki.

These selections were made on the basis of careful pre-evaluations of each potential member of the class. Jessie was an overachieving, slightly fearful herding dog who was strongly driven to protect her owner from the mere presence of other dogs. Schmaal was a graceful, athletic sighthound, who routinely responded to other dog with aggression, though the stress of a training class made her act aloof, almost to the point of catatonia. Her stress level was so high in class, in fact, that getting her to eat treats was a major accomplishment.

Kito the Akita was previously abused and had been attacked by dogs before; he seemed to go on the defensive with other dogs due to apprehension about being attacked. In general, it seemed he had a lot of issues to sort out. Beau, however, was the greatest concern. He had been attacking dogs all of his life, enjoyed being a bully (all 120 pounds of him), and was on a restricted diet due to problems with his digestive system. He also had been through punishment-based training to try to control his aggression.

Food is an important part of a successful Growl Class. Instructors use positive methods to reduce the dogs' stress and to teach them that having other dogs around is a "good" thing. This can only be accomplished with reinforcement and reward. Food is a primary reinforcer that can be delivered quickly and easily, so its use is critical in getting a dog to think positively about a stimulus (the presence of other dogs) that has previously been perceived as a negative.

In this particular class, the use of food as a reward was problematic for two of the dogs (Beau had digestive problems, and Schmaal was too stressed to eat). This presented additional challenges.

First Session

Dogs are not allowed to interact in the first session of a Growl Class. Instead, certain exercises are practiced and homework assigned so that the dogs are more responsive to their owners before their first interaction in Class Two. Students and their dogs spread out around the training area—with as much distance between them as possible. People and dogs are seated on blankets or rugs on the ground.

The first class features an in-depth discussion of dog behavior, aggression, and canine body language. Each owner describes his dog's history of aggression, and the kind of behavior he anticipates from his dog in the class setting. We analyze the body language that each of the dogs displays, discuss its likely meaning, and make predictions about the dogs' behaviors during the interaction to come. It is important from the very beginning of the first class that owners begin to develop their skills in reading dog body language so they know when and how to intervene appropriately.

Next, owners discuss their feelings about their dogs and about the class. It is normal for owners to be apprehensive. It's explained that the dogs will not be allowed to hurt each other, and that one goal of the class is to allow dogs to interact safely so that they can learn appropriate body language and social behavior around each other.

Then, the work begins. Unlike regular training classes, where the instructor is upbeat, speaks cheerfully, and moves quickly, Growl Classes are almost like meditation sessions. The first exercise is intended to lower the stress levels of dogs and owners by doing relaxation exercises—massage on a rug or blanket for the dogs, and deep breathing for the owners.

Next, dogs and owners learn an "Off" exercise , which means that if dogs give a "hard glare" to another dog they are asked to "Off" and are given a Click! and treat when they look away from the other dog. They also get clicks and treats for "soft" glances (and tail wags!) at other dogs, and lots of clicks and treats for paying attention to their owners. The purpose of this is to teach them that the presence of other dogs is a good thing—they get lots of treats when other dogs are around.

As anticipated, Beau had the most difficulty with this critically important exercise. Not only was he very committed to the hard stare that signals the pre-launch phase of an all-out attack, but the treats his owners used—his regular dinner kibble—were not nearly attractive enough to distract him from his seek-and-destroy missions. We finally began to have some success with Beau in Week Four, when we started rubbing meaty treats on our hands and let him lick the flavor off for his reward.

Another exercise taught in the first class is the "Gotcha!," a positive cue (with treat reward) for a grab on a dog's collar, which becomes necessary when intervening in a scuffle.

The class practiced fitting muzzles on the dogs, and did one-at-a-time leash-walking around the training area; owners practiced their tone of voice (calm and upbeat, not panicked or commanding) for use with the "Off" cue. Relaxation exercises ended the class. Dog and owner pairs were instructed to leave calmly, one at a time, to avoid confrontations at the door.

Relaxation Exercises

Relaxation exercises are an important part of Growl Class success. Lowering the dogs' (and owners') levels of anxiety at the beginning and end of each class contributres greatly to calm behavior and positive interactions during class. It also teaches dogs and owners valuable skills to greatly calm behavior and positive interactions to use when they find themselves in stressful situations outside of class.

Owners are taught deep breathing and voice control. They practice the verbal part of the "Gotcha" and "Off" exercises (described on the following pages) without the dog present, so they can learn to say the cue words calmly and brightly, without betraying their own anxiety. If they can control their own emotions, they can avoid heightening their dogs' stress levels.

Also recommended is teaching the dogs a verbal "Relax" cue, which includes having them lie on their sides. This is a naturally relaxing position, especially when accompanied by gentle stroking, massage, and use of calming acupressure points.

An owner can use this anytime she senses her dog becoming aroused by the presence of another dog—assuming the other dog is under control and will not approach or attack the dog being worked in the "Relax" position.

In time, just the use of the word "Relax" can elicit a conditioned response that can calm a dog at the beginning stages of arousal.

Clockwise, from top:
1) Josie is staring intensely at a strange dog in her yard, ignoring attempts to get her attention.

2) With the use of the "Relax" cue, gentle words and touch, Josie begins to settle but is still conscious of the other dog.

3) Now she has removed her attention from the other dog and is focusing on the instructor, the massage, and the petting.

4) Now fully relaxed, Josie lies flat with her head down; her rapid panting has subsided into calm, deep breathing.

"Gotcha!"

This is a safety exercise and one that is beneficial for all dogs to know, not just Growl Class participants. Most dogs, at some time in their lives, will have someone grab them by the collar. Many dogs find this a frightening, threatening experience and some response with a defensive bite.

Most dogs are much more comfortable having their collars grasped under their chin rather than over their head. The back of the neck is a sensitive trigger point for dominance aggression. Train yourself to reach under, not over your dog's head to grasp his collar.

By teaching them that a collar grab is a positive thing, we desensitize them to the movement, minimize the likelihood of bites, and make it safer for us to intervene in a Growl Class interaction.

Start this exercise (see opposite page) by determining the dog's comfort level. Some dogs are fearful of an empty hand approaching their face. Others are tolerant of collar touching until a hand reaches over the back of the neck. Always start where the dog is comfortable and work from there.

Week Two

Every class from the second week forward starts and ends with the relaxation exercises learned in the first class. Then owners put the muzzles on and do some calm on-leash walking/attention exercises. At first, three dogs sat while one walked, while getting lots of positive reinforcement from her owner for calm behavior as she passed the other dogs. Then they did "pass-bys," where two dogs pass each other walking on leash, again with lots of treats for good behavior. The challenges of Beau's and Schmaal's food restrictions became apparent early in this exercise.

After the relaxation and leash exercises, the first off-leash interaction was conducted. Owners were told when to release their dogs—and then to simply stand back out of the way. Confrontations between the dogs was likely, but the muzzles prevent injury.

The first off-leash interaction was a high anxiety time: "If there is a problem," students were cautioned, "let the instructor handle it." Everyone took several deep breaths, and then released their dogs.

First (muzzled) interaction

Surprisingly, little Jessie was the first aggressor. She flew out from

Clockwise, from top: Begin by softly saying "Gotcha" and touching the dog's collar in the least threatening position, under the jaw, then feeding a treat. If that is too threatening, simply offer your hand with the Gotcha!" and feed a treat without touching. As the dog gets comfortable with the under-the-chin collar touch, repeat the exercise by circling your hand over the dog's head as you say "Gotcha!" and give a treat. If he tolerates that well, add the collar grasp at the back of the neck. Make sure your dog is comfortable with one phase before proceeding to the next. If he shrinks away from you at any point, you may have progressed too quickly. Go back to the level where the dog was comfortable and practice for a while before proceeding, more slowly this time. Practice when the dog is not looking at you and is not expecting it. If you always give a treat for the "Gotcha!", over time your dog should become more confident, not flinch from the "grab" and eagerly walk into the pressure in anticipation of the treat.

behind her owner at Schmaal, who wandered by too closely. This started a free-for-all, with the most intense aggression, as expected, between Beau and Kito.

Jessie and Schmaal disengaged fairly quickly, while Beau and Kito trounced each other for several minutes before calling a truce, after which everyone breathed a sigh of relief.

The dogs wandered around the training area, glaring but not attacking. They were called, rewarded, leashes put back on, muzzles removed—and settled down for more relaxation and debriefing. Yes, it was scary, but a relief to see that the muzzles worked, and that the fighters stopped quickly, and of their own accord.

However, in the next class, the fighting would not be allowed to continue to its own conclusion. Rather, the "Off" interrupter would be used to try to intervene pre-launch (with a big click and reward if the dogs succeeded), and "Gotcha" to intervene post-launch if necessary.

Owners were instructed to practice "Off" and "Gotcha" for at least 20 minutes per day, so that the dogs would attain a high level of responsiveness by the next class.

Third Class

In the third week, Jessie's owner reported she was making great progress, passing other dogs on the street without giving them the evil eye, and responding nicely to "Off" and rewards. Schmaal, also, was doing surprisingly well. Although she still disdained treats in class, she would eat them out in the "real world."

However, Beau and Kito were cause for concern. Even during relaxation exercises Beau glowered at Kito from the opposite corner of the room.

Despite pleas to Beau's owners to find some other kind of high-value treat, they still fed him only kibble.

The class warmed up with by-passes; Jessie and Schmaal got to do theirs without muzzles. Then, with all four dogs muzzled, we tried for some controlled interaction.

The dogs were released. Beau and Kito launched for each other; Jessie and Schmaal wanted to join in but responded to their owners when called back. Lots of rewards and treats for that!

Meanwhile the two big bruisers seriously went at it. We looked for an opportunity to intervene with an "Off" and a "Gotcha" and retired to our relaxation rugs.

Next, Jessie and Schmaal had an opportunity to interact without "the boys." Muzzles on, there was only a brief threat from Jessie — and it was over almost before it began.

Class Four and Five

Kito didn't show up for the next class. It was disheartening, and it put a crimp in the program. We did our basic exercises with the three remaining dogs, and tried an off-leash interaction with all the dogs muzzled. Beau behaved well with just the girls present. His owners learned how to rub meat flavoring on their hands and the kibble treats, to get Beau more engaged in the reward process. It-worked for the wife, who learned to combine the treat reward with upbeat verbal praise, but Beau still ignored the husband's boring treats and monotone voice.

This session went so well that after the three-dog interaction Beau was put back on his relaxation rug, and Jessie and Schmaal's muzzles removed. With calm, relaxed off-leash walking, owners nearby, both dogs did beautifully. Jessie was aware of the other dog but she stayed under control; Schmaal just pretended Jessie wasn't there. All agreed Beau was not ready for off-leash interaction without his muzzle.

Kito returned for the fifth class, which seemed to renew the animosity between the two big males. Beau would not respond to his "Off" and "Gotcha" exercises, and the off-leash interaction between the two was not productive; Beau simply wanted to bully Kito unmercifully. Kito was removed from the training area to repeat the previous week's success with Beau and the two girls, but he was too aroused from his interaction with Kito, and jumped on Jessie. For the boys, the focus for the rest of the classes was "on-leash" behaviors.

Jessie and Schmaal continued to progress with off-leash and off-muzzle work. Jessie's owner became adept at reading Jessie's body language and pre-empting any kind of scuffle with the "Off" cue.

Final Class

Kito dropped out—a big disappointment because Kito had much more potential than he was allowed to develop.

We began our last class with relaxation exercises, talked about our goals and how we felt the dogs had done throughout the class. It was agreed Jessie was the star of the class—just the right type of dog to benefit the most from a Difficult Dog class: Bonded to her owner, food motivated, responsive, and committed to doing her job. She just needed to have her job description rewritten slightly. Her owner reported that while Jessie was not yet 100 percent reliable around other dogs she was much improved. Now her owner has confidence in her own awareness of canine body language and her improved control over her dog. Now she can take Jessie places and give her considerably more freedom than in the past.

Schmaal's owner was pleased with her progress. While she was nowhere near ready to turn Schmaal loose on the beach with a pack of dogs, she was much more confident in her ability to get Schmaal to respond to her when necessary.

Beau was the biggest disappointment. At Week Six he was still looking for someone to bully. His eight-year history of dog aggression, along with his owners' failure to find a suitably enticing reward, proved to be insurmountable obstacles. While he was marginally better behaved on leash around other dogs, and did respond to the relaxation exercises, Beau still had a long way to go.

There is a crying need to help dogs remember how to be part of a pack. Dog-aggressive breeds, poorly socialized pups, and dogs encouraged or allowed to be aggressive with each other are a result of human, not canine, failure. Dogs are designed to live and work together in relative harmony, and we have botched the plan.

But for many dogs it is not too late. If you have a dog who wants to eat other dogs for breakfast, find your nearest positive reinforcement trainer (who will use treats, praise and other rewards rather than choke or pinch collars) and ask for assistance. If you're lucky, he/she may start a Growl Class soon.

"Off!" Part I

"Off" is another exercise that has applications far beyond the Growl Class. "Off" means "Whatever you are paying attention to, I want you to leave it alone."

It can apply to the hors d'oeurves on the coffee table, the skunk in the back yard, the dead seal on the beach...or the growling Rottweiler that you and your dog are about to pass on the sidewalk. It is a simple exercise to teach, and most dogs learn it very quickly.

By rewarding them with an exceptionally valuable treat for looking away from the forbidden object, they quickly learn to turn to you when they hear the "Off" cue.

You must program them that what you are going to give them is infinitely more desirable than the object they are being asked to ignore. Most dogs can learn to ignore treats on the ground directly in front of them in just one short training session.

Clockwise, from top left: Josie is offered a treat in the trainer's closed fist and told "Off!"—once only, in an upbeat tone.The intent is not to intimidate her away from the treat, but to help her make a correct choice to a positive verbal cue. She licks and paws the hand, trying to get the treat. 2) She continues to try to get the treat. The trainer wait s patiently, without repeating "Off!"—so that Josie will take responsibility for her behavior—not be "nagged" into it. 3) Confused, Josie pulls her nose back from the treat. 4) Immediately, the trainer Clicks! or says "Yes!" to mark the good behavior, and feeds Josie a treat from the other hand. This exercise is repeated until Josie pulls her nose away from the forbidden treat the instant the trainer says "Off," and continues to leave it alone when the trainer opens her hand with the treat in full view. If Josie dives for the open hand the trainer closes her fist, and goes "Click!" and treats only when when Josie pulls away.

"Off!" Part II

This is the beginning of the practical application of "Off." Create an "Off" Course by setting up several small piles of treats in an open area. Pavement is best—treat piles in grass are too hard to see. The more you practice the more reliable your dog will become in real world situations.

One tip: if your dog is having trouble with this, start by using really boring treats on the ground and wonderful ones in your hand, so the reward for doing the "Off!" is infinitely better than grabbing the pile.

Clockwise from top left: Josie sees the treat pile and heads for it. The trainer says "Off!" andgently restrains her so she can't reach it. Then she invites her to come with a tasty treat. As soon as Josie turns away from the pile she gets a "Yes!" or a "Click!" and the treat. 2) On the second pass, she resonds immediately to the "Off!" cue, and 3) Gets a "Click!" and a jackpot—a whole handful of treats for her wonderful behavior.

"Off!" with Another Dog

In Growl Class, all dogs are relaxed on their rugs while one dog is walked on leash at a far enough distance from the others to avoid triggering aggression. When the walking dog glances at another dog, the owner gives the "Off!" cue and rewards the "Off!" response.

As the dogs become skilled at this, the "Off!" is used during other exercises and interactions, and can also reward her for bringing her attention back to you. Doing this with non-threatening interactions will increase the reliability of her response when faced with potentially aggressive situations in real life. If she notices another dog, ask her to "Off!" and reward her when she brings her attention back to you.

From top: Katie eyes a strange dog at her house with suspicion. If this were a "Growl" Class, Rupert's owner would be kneeling next to him doing relaxation exercises. Next, Katie makes a little rush straight for Rupert. Her owner quickly gives her the "Off!" cue and invites her away with a treat. When she responds she gets the "Click!" and reward. By the third pass, Katie turns away from the other dog on the "Off!" cue, and looks for her reward. By the; fifth pass she doesn't evenbother to look at Rupert. Mission accomplished!"

12

Treating Noise-Phobic Dogs

Desensitizing a dog with noise phobias is possible, but takes time and patience. Don't look for the quick and easy fix.

Once upon a time, a 12-week-old Australian Kelpie puppy went to a county fair with her owner who stayed to the very end to watch the evening's fireworks display. With the first deafening pyrotechnic boom and ensuing brilliant lights, Keli urinated in her owner's lap and struggled frantically to escape. Despite efforts to comfort her as the show continued, she was in a total, unmitigated panic. It was a perfect way to create a noise-phobic dog. For the rest of her 14 years, Keli trembled violently in fear and crawled under the bed during thunderstorms and when 4th of July and New Year firecrackers rocked the tranquility of the neighborhood.

Preventing Noise Phobias

Many behaviorists and dog trainers believe that puppies go through a so-called "fear imprinting" period sometime between the ages of eight to 20 weeks, when they learn what is safe in the big wide world, and what is not. Exposure to traumatic stimuli during this period can have long-lasting effects, as the fireworks did with Keli.

The same exposure after this critical period might temporarily frighten a dog, but is much less likely to do permanent damage to a dog's psyche. Obviously then, the first step in dealing with noise phobias is prevention. During this "fear imprinting" period of a young pup's life, it is imperative to take extra precautions to see that she isn't traumatized by unusually loud or sudden noises.

Even later on in a dog's life, it is important to avoid experiences, such as confining the dog near a noise-producing object, that might trigger an unhealthy fear of loud noises. And there may actually be a genetic predisposition for the development of fearful behaviors, which would help to explain why one dog can tolerate repeated noisy stimuli with impunity, while another needs only one exposure to the same stimulus to develop a severe behavior problem.

But what do we do about the thousands of noise-phobic dogs for whom prevention is no longer an option? The damage has already been done. Are they doomed, like Keli, to spend the rest of their lives hiding under the bed whenever storm clouds gather?

It is a serious concern. Animal shelters universally report that July 5th and January 1st are the two busiest days of the year in their kennels, caring for dogs who escaped the night before. Fear-induced adrenaline causes dogs to scale fences that would normally be more than adequate to keep them safely confined. Some even go through plate-glass windows and dig through doors in their frantic attempts to escape the torment of the noise.

Noise-phobic dogs, often labeled "gun shy," may react to firecrackers, gunshots, cars backfiring, cap guns, wood chopping, falling pots and pans, and any other loud noise. But by far the most common stimulus that triggers noise phobia in dogs is the thunderstorm.

Thunderstorms offer a number of potential fear-producing stimuli, including the noise of thunder, wind and rain, flashes of lightning, changes in atmospheric pressure, ionization, and storm-related odors.

Treatments

Fortunately, there are ways to desensitize noise-phobic dogs. It takes time and a real commitment on the part of the dog owner to follow through on a noise desensitization program, but such programs, if followed faithfully, do have a good chance of succeeding.

Whileall the aforementioned stimuli may play a role in thunderstorm phobias, the most overpowering and easiest of them to replicate for modification work is the noise component.

The two most common approaches to behavior modification involve either desensitization and counter-conditioning, or flooding and habituation (see "Behavioral Definitions," next page). Medications have been used in noise phobia treatment with mixed success. While they may help to calm and control a dog during a storm and prevent self-inflicted injury, they seem to have little long-term effect on the dog's fear. Also, drugs may actually inhibit a dog's ability to learn that the storm is not frightening.

Desensitization/counter-conditioning and flooding/habituation are opposite approaches; one can't do both at the same time. Flooding can be extremely traumatic, and once embarked upon must be followed to its conclusion in order to be successful. This can take many hours, and if the session is stopped before the dog relaxes and accepts the noise, it is likely to just make the problem worse – the dog may think that it was the fearful behavior that finally succeeded in making the noise stop. Flooding is commonly used in the treatment of human fears and phobias, but much less so in dogs.

Desensitization and counter-conditioning, on the other hand, are used together frequently and successfully to overcome canine fears. We can't use real storms in a desensitization program. Real storms happen too quickly to allow for the gradual increase in intensity that is necessary for desensitization to succeed. However, we can create artificial, controllable thunderstorms through the creative use of stereo equipment, recordings of thunder, strobe lights (to simulate lightning) and sprinklers or hoses to create the sound of rain on the window or roof.

Behavioral Definitions

- *Phobia: A non-useful, counter-productive fear response that is out of proportion to the real level of threat posed by the stimulus.*

- *Counter-conditioning: A technique by which an animal is conditioned to respond in ways that are incompatible with an undesirable response, by gradually presenting the feared stimulus while the animal is engaged in a pleasurable activity (such as eating food). Ideally the stimulus is presented at a level that does not evoke a fear reaction at any time. (Usually performed simultaneously with desensitization.)*

- *Desensitization: A technique used to reduce fear responses in a step-by-step process by exposing the animal initially to non-fearful stimuli and gradually increasing the intensity of the stimuli without evoking a fear response.*

■ *Flooding: A fear-removal technique whereby an animal is continuously exposed to a full-strength fear-causing stimulus until the animal stops exhibiting the fearful behavior. The stimulus is not removed until some time after the animal has completely relaxed. At the end of the session the animal is experiencing the full-strength stimulus in a non-fearful state of mind.*

■ *Habituation: The decrease or loss of response to a fear-inducing stimulus solely as the result of repeated exposure to that stimulus without the use of pleasant or aversive associations (rewards or punishments)*

The Desensitization Program

Begin your behavior modification program by finding a recording (or combination of recording and other stimuli) that causes your dog to react fearfully. Thunderstorm recordings on tape or CD are available at most music outlets. As soon as the dog begins to show fear of the stimuli, turn them off. You don't want to evoke a full fear response; you just want to find the level at which your dog begins to respond.

Once the dog is totally relaxed again you can begin the training program. Start by playing the recording below the level that would evoke a fearful response. This may be at a level that you cannot even hear. Remember that your dog's hearing is infinitely better than yours. After five minutes or so, increase the sound slightly. (This is the desensitization part.) While your dog is still calm, feed him absolutely wonderful treats – roast beef or steak, fried chicken skins, or anything else that your dog would normally do backflips for. (This is the counter-conditioning part.) You want him to think that absolutely wonderful things happen when thunderstorm noises occur.

Be generous with totally terrific treats, petting, and praise, and keep the sound at each level for several minutes before gradually increasing the volume again. At some point, your dog will start to exhibit a mild, fearful reaction. (If it is not mild, you have increased the volume too quickly.) Watch for panting, pacing, clinging to you, and other signs of tension.

When this happens you have two choices. You can either immediately turn the volume back down, or wait and see if the dog habituates to that level of intensity. If the reaction is truly mild and you have been very gradually increasing the volume, it is preferable to wait for habituation.

Keep the volume at this level for a considerable period of time before increasing the volume again ("considerable period of time" depends on the individual dog). As soon as the dog relaxes – when the signs of stress go away – resume treat-feeding and petting.

Move Forward Slowly

It is important not to play the recording too loudly or to increase the volume too quickly. This is the most common mistake made in desensitization programs – increasing the stimuli level too rapidly. It is very important not to evoke a fear response that does not habituate during the session; this would be a major step backward. Be patient. While the first few sessions may proceed slowly, typically subsequent sessions will go much faster. It often takes only three to five sessions to move past the initial volume level at which the dog first reacted fearfully. This can be accomplished in less than a week.

Once your dog accepts loud thunderstorm noises, reduce the volume and add the other stimuli, one at a time, until he is comfortable with the entire package. Each time you add a new stimulus, reduce the intensity of the others and gradually increase them again, one at a time.

You will also want to change locations from time to time, so the dog accepts the stimuli package in any room of the house. Later on, the onset of the artificial storm should occur outside of formal training sessions – at first perhaps while the dog is playing with a favorite toy, or eating dinner, then at random times.

When your dog is comfortable with storm noises in all of these situations, you can set your storm on a timer to play at very low levels for very short intervals (at first) when you are not home. Remember: Every time you change an aspect of the exercise you must reduce the intensity of each element of the stimulus package.

For noises other than storms, it is a matter of finding an adequate artificial replication of the offending noise and any other relevant stimuli that can be incorporated into a similar program.

A Shocking Theory

Some people believe that it is the build-up of static electricity (and resultant static shocks to the dog) that occurs during a thunderstorm that makes many dogs develop an extreme fear of storms.

This would explain why some dogs hide in bathtubs or wedge themselves behind toilets when a storm hits. Their contact with the porcelain plumbing fixtures is thought to ground them and protect them from shocks. Many storm-phobic dogs are much more calm if they are allowed to "ride out" the storm in a car – maybe because the car protects them from the storm sounds as well as from static shocks.

Some owners report success with laundry no-cling strips. Rubbing these sheets over the dog can also prevent static shocks. It is not an unreasonable theory. The intensity of many dogs' reactions to storms is comparable to the extreme reaction often seen by dogs who are subjected to shocks from electronic training collars. Driving your dog around in a car during a storm, or rubbing him with laundry no-cling sheets are easy and inexpensive solutions to try.

While not every noise-phobic dog can be successfully desensitized, behaviorists report a fair degree of success with desensitization programs like the one described above. This is good news to the owners of the thousands of noise-phobic dogs that suffer through thunderstorms and other fear-inducing sounds.

How Long Does It Take?

Studies indicate that frequent, long desensitization/counter-conditioning sessions (30-45 minutes) are more effective than multiple short ones. Mild to moderate phobias may be successfully treated in just a few weeks. Severe cases can take longer—a month or more is not unusual; and unfortunately, sometimes they never come around—studies of desensitization programs for extremely noise-phobic dogs are not very encouraging. Many of these dogs don't respond. However, this may be because the dogs weren't being desensitized to the right stimulus. It is important to mimic as many of the elements of the package of thunderstorm stimuli as possible for the greatest chance of success.

It is beneficial to accomplish desensitization as quickly as possible. If a real storm occurs during the training process and traumatizes the dog it can set the training back. Where storms are seasonal, it makes sense to start and complete the program during the "off" season. Because the desensitization can apparently fade with time, it is also a good idea to refresh the training once or twice a month.

13

Does Your Dog Bite?

Biting is a natural, normal dog behavior, but every dog has his "bite threshold."

The trainer had been playing with the 120-pound, confident, intact male Rottweiler for more than 45 minutes. He sat next to him and leaned happily against his leg. Without thinking, the trainer bent down and reached across the back of the dog's neck to scratch behind his ear.

In a split second the dog's eyes went cold and the trainer felt, rather than heard, the rumble of a growl from deep within his throat. He whirled away from the Rottweiler's massive jaws just in time to catch the bite in the padded shoulder of his jacket, rather than his face. He stood perfectly still, heart thudding, legs weak, waiting to see what the dog would do next. But the dog sat back down, smiled a big Rottweiler grin and wagged his stump of a tail.

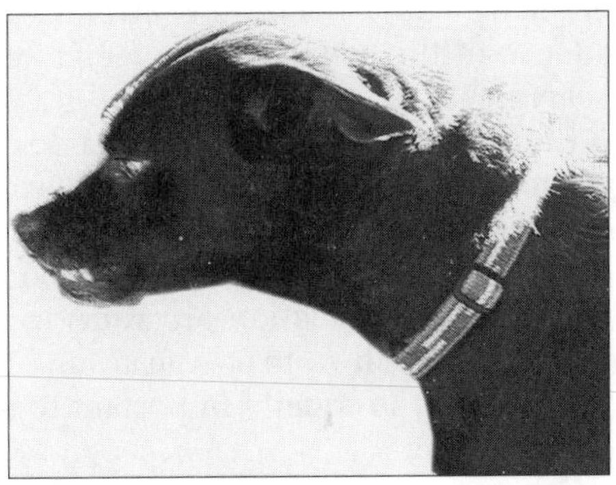

A dog who signals his intent to bite, like the one above, is actually a far safer companion than a dog who has been punished for this behavior and then learned to suppress it. When exposed to enough stress, the latter will inevitably bite—probably without warning.

"No hard feelings," he was saying, "as long as you mind your place."

The professional dog trainer should have known better. The dog's sensibilities as a dominant male had been offended by the trainer-having the audacity to reach over the back of his neck, a serious challenge in dog-speak. Only luck and quick reactions saved him-from being badly bitten in the face. A child, a senior, any unsuspecting person in this situation could easily have ended up at the nearest emergency room, headed for the plastic surgeon.

Common Problem

Biting is a natural, normal dog behavior, something we tend to forget. All dogs can bite; many do and all dogs are potential biters. This is why dog bites are so prevalent—statistically, the number one health problem for children in this country, surpassing measles, mumps, and whooping cough combined, according to Jeffrey Sacks, MD, of the National Centers for Disease Control in Atlanta.

The CDC estimates that some 4.7 million persons were bitten by dogs in 1996. Of these, approximately 830,000 of the bites required medical attention, up from 585,000 in 1986. Another chilling example: A 1994 survey of 3,238 Pennsylvania school children determined that by the 12th grade, 46 percent of students had been bitten by a dog.. Between 1980 and 1996, 304 people died from dog attacks in this country, an average of 19 dog-related fatalities per year

Children are the most common dog bite victims due to their size, vulnerability, and tendency to move quickly and make strange noises, especially when excited or frightened.

A great deal has been written about how to avoid being bitten, and there are education programs in schools across the country to teach children how to be safe around dogs. While this effort is commendable, it is equally important to address the canine end of the bite equation.

Anyone who has ever owned a dog who has bitten a person knows the stress of living with a known biter, the guilt of seeing stitches in a child's face, and the agony that comes with making the painful decision to have a four-footed friend euthanized rather than risk injury to another human.

If we had a better understanding of how our dogs' minds work, we could prevent many bites from happening, and successfully rehabilitate many dogs who have become problem biters through mismanagement and inappropriate training.

The Bite Threshold

According to Canadian author and dog trainer Jean Donaldson in her excellent book, *Culture Clash*, dogs, like humans, have a breaking point beyond which, if pushed, they respond with aggression. She calls this the "bite threshold." Dogs also have thresholds for other threat behaviors such as growling, snarling, and snapping.

Anything that stresses the dog is a risk factor. Risk factors vary from one dog to the next, but can include things like loud noises, children, anything the dog associates with punishment (a leather strap, rolled-up newspaper, choke chain), and anything to which the dog has not been adequately socialized, such as strange men, umbrellas, odd hats—you name it.

...DOGS, LIKE HUMANS, HAVE A BREAKING POINT BEYOND WHICH, IF PUSHED, THEY RESPOND WITH AGGRESSION.

The list of possible risk factors is endless. Any one risk factor may be enough of a stimulus to cross a particular dog's bite threshold, but in many cases it is a combination of factors that join together to push a dog past his limit.

For example, let's say Rascal is not overly fond of small children, he's afraid of loud noises, and a little bit protective of his toys. One day the owner's two-year-old granddaughter is visiting during a thunderstorm, and crawls over to Rascal, who is lying in the corner on the floor next to his favorite toy. Rascal, who has always in the past just avoided the toddler, is on edge from the thunder, feels cornered and can't get away, and sees the girl reaching out toward his most valuable possession. "Without warning," Rascal lunges and grabs the little girl's face. The combination of risk factors has pushed him past his bite threshold.

In fact, there was plenty of warning, if someone had just been able to recognize Rascal's nervousness with each of the individual risk factors and understood that putting them all together placed the child at a significant risk of being attacked.

Classifications of Aggression

We tend to think of aggression as being one of two types: either dominance aggression, where the dog thinks he's the pack leader and bites to get his way; or submission aggression, also known as fear aggression, where the shy, timid dog bites when he feels cornered or threatened.

In reality, the analysis of aggression is much more complex than this; there are more than a dozen different identifiable classifications of aggression, each with different triggers and approaches to modifying the aggressive behavior. Most dogs who have a problem with inappropriate aggression display more than one type. A competent trainer or behaviorist will be able to accurately identify and work with all of the various types of aggression that a dog may manifest in order to effectively resolve the complete problem.

The Positive Approach

There was a time when the generally accepted method of correcting a dog's aggression was to be more aggressive than the dog. If your dog growled at you when you jerked on her leash or tried to force her to lie down, you were instructed to "pop" her under the chin with a closed fist. If she snapped at you in response, you might have been told to do a "scruff shake" or "alpha roll." If she continued to fight you, your trainer might have taken the leash from you to "hang" or "helicopter" the dog. These techniques are as abusive as they sound – dogs have been blinded, permanently brain-damaged, and even killed by these methods. Even so, some trainers continue to use and defend the use of hanging and helicoptering even today.

But progressive, humane trainers have come to understand that aggression begets aggression. Many dogs respond to a physical correction by escalating their own aggression in their own self-defense. Unless you are willing and able to out-escalate the dog, the dog "wins" the fight and the aggression worsens. Even if you succeed in overpowering the dog, all you have done is suppress the signs of aggression; the risk factors for the aggressive behavior are still there. You have simply taught the dog not to growl or snap in warning.

When you suppress the warning signs of aggression – the growling and snarling – you actually increase the risk of a serious bite, since the aggression is then more likely to erupt into a full-scale attack without giving you the chance to be warned off by the growl.

Desensitize The Dog

A far better approach is to desensitize the dog to the risk factors, that is, to change the way he thinks about them. The fewer risk factors a particular dog has, the less likely they are to join in a combination powerful enough to push him over his threshold and cause him to bite. For instance, if we can get Rascal to think that having children around is a good thing, he will no longer be nervous when they are near, and the presence of children can be eliminated as a risk factor.

We start out by discontinuing the practice of punishing him when children are around. If he growls at a child and we jerk on his leash or smack him, we have reinforced his belief that bad things happen when children are present. If we exclude him from the family when the grandkids visit, we also teach him that bad things happen when children are present—he gets exiled from the pack. If, instead, we can consistently make good things happen when kids are around, Rascal will begin to look forward to their presence instead of fearing them.

We can accomplish this through the use of a reward marker, such as the Click! of a clicker, or the word Yes!, which we have already taught the dog to associate with a tasty treat. You might begin your desensitization process by finding a location where children are far enough away that Rascal can see them but not feel threatened by them (it helps to employ children whom you know and can instruct to stay away). When Rascal notices the children, Click! the clicker and feed him a treat. Each time he glances at the children and remains calm, Click! and treat. This will begin to teach him that seeing children (and remaining calm) is a good thing – children mean treats!

Dominant stare or hard concentration? Without knowing the dog well, it would be unwise to stare back or to push farther forward into the dog's personal space. The safest tack would be to interpret this look as a warning.

Gradually move closer, continuing to Click! and treat for

calm behavior. Don't push your luck, however. If you notice the tiniest sign of nervousness on Rascal's part as you near the children, stop and calmly retreat. If children come toward you, attracted by the dog, use a clear, firm, but calm tone and tell them to stay back!

When employing a desensitization program, you need to avoid triggering the behavior you are trying to eliminate. Getting the dog too stressed and forcing him to growl or snap at a child would be a serious setback to your program. Watch closely, and stop at the first sign of discomfort. If you have moved forward in small enough steps you may be able to pause for a moment, wait for calm behavior to return, and Click! and treat the dog for making a good choice of behaviors. If you have been impatient and moved forward too quickly, you may have to back up to find the point where the dog's calm behavior returns, and Click! and reward him there. It is always better to move forward slowly and end on a positive note than have to back up and repair damage.

Once you are close enough, and assuming your dog is still calm, you can ask the children to toss treats to the dog, so he starts realizing that good things actually come from the children themselves. (It may take days, weeks, or even longer to get a dog who is very fearful of children to this point.) Ask the children not to stare into the dog's eyes, as this is a strong threat for a dog, and be sure to do this exercise, at least at first, with children you trust to be calm and not act fearful themselves. Over time, you should start to see signs – wagging tail, bright eyes, perked ears—that your dog is eagerly anticipating his encounters with kids instead of fearing them.

Prevention Preferred

It is far easier to prevent undesirable behavior than it is to correct it. A desensitization program can take anywhere from several weeks, to months, even years, depending on the intensity of the dog's discomfort with the risk factor, and the owner's or trainer's skill. And while you may succeed in desensitizing the dog in the above example to, say, the child factor, you haven't even begun to address his protection aggression over his favorite toy.

If you start when your dog is a puppy and you raise him right, you can avoid a lot of the headache and heartache of risk factors through proper socialization. Socialization means getting used to environmental elements through exposure.

In the wild, a puppy is naturally exposed to the elements of the world during the first several months of puppyhood. Anything new he encounters after that is cause for alarm, or at least for extreme caution. The same thing is true of our domesticated puppies. If you make an effort to expose pups to lots of different stimuli during the first five months of their lives, they will grow up with a much shorter list of risk factors. Of course, the exposure must be positive – exposure to traumatizing stimuli during this same period will make the list longer!

So, if you want a dog to be comfortable around children, men, odd hats, etc., you better make darn sure that he meets a lot of kids and men and people wearing odd hats who are nice to him and feed him treats before he is five months old. Renowned trainer Ian Dunbar suggests that people hold occasional "puppy parties" for this purpose; the diverse attendees ALL wear funny hats and act strangely, and they all take turns praising and feeding the puppy treats!

If you want your puppy to get along with other dogs, give him plenty of opportunities to play with other puppies and appropriate (non-aggressive) adult dogs while he is young. If you want him to not be possessive of his food and toys, spend time gently showing him that you can take toys and food away and give them back, or that if you approach while he is eating you may give him more food, or better food than what he already has. Do this without punishment, and he will learn to associate pleasant things with each of these stimuli.

Fearful Puppies

Some puppies are born more fearful than others. It is especially important to take the time to socialize these shy guys, or they can turn into serious fear biters. Because of the gap that can occur between protection from maternal antibodies and puppyhood vaccines, some veterinarians counsel their clients to keep puppies confined at home until at least the age of four months. Unfortunately, while these pups may never die of distemper or parvovirus, they risk losing their homes, and perhaps their lives, because of the socialization that they miss during their critical learning period. Far more dogs are euthanized due to behavior problems caused by lack of socialization and training than puppies who contracted diseases from exposure to other dogs.

Many training classes now start puppies as young as 10 weeks as long as they as they are properly vaccinated, in an effort to provide socialization and early training for the youngsters. These pups never have a chance to learn wrong behaviors, since they learn the right ones from a very early age—as long as the trainer uses positive, non-punitive training methods and no choke chains.

IT IS FAR EASIER TO PREVENT UNDESIRABLE BEHAVIOR THAN IT IS TO CORRECT IT.

Get Help

If you have a dog who already has lots of risk factors, seek help from a competent professional soon, rather than later. Don't wait until a tragedy occurs to recognize your dog's potential to bite, and don't fall into the denial trap. If your dog reacts to a lot of risk factors, or reacts strongly to any one particular factor, likelihood is high that sooner or later he will be pushed past his bite threshold.

Remember, all dogs can bite. When you interview trainers, check their credentials, and be relentless in your questioning about their methods.

And what of the Rottweiler who wanted to eat the trainer? He wasn't a "client;" the trainer was there on his ranch with a humane officer to investigate a complaint of horse neglect, so there was no chance to work with him to modify his behavior. And he is still out there—a time bomb, running loose on the ranch, that sooner or later will explode in the face of someone who doesn't turn away in time. There are far too many such time bombs out there. Don't let your dog be one of them.

14

The Timid Dog

Dogs need to be exposed early and often to a variety of "outside world" experiences—for their own safety and yours.

Dogs aren't born full-fledged "man's best friends." As with all baby animals, there is a period of time in their lives when they must learn about the world in order to survive. This critical period is a window of opportunity for socializatin—a time when puppies learn what is safe and good and what is not. Opinions differ as to how long the window is open, but it falls somewhere in the period between four and 20 weeks. After the window closes, anything not previously identified as safe will automatically fall into the unsafe category. Dogs must be socialized to the human world during this time, or they will forever be fearful of—or, at the very least, anxious about—new people, sights, and sounds.

Socialization: Learned, Not Innate

Dogs who are well-socialized receive lots of gentle human contact and handling from the time their eyes open on into adulthood. Guide Dogs For The Blind and other service dog organizations who must produce the calmest, most socialized dogs possible send their puppies to live with 4-H families, where the participants try to take their service puppies with them everywhere they go. As they get older (eight to 20 weeks) they are given careful exposure to other stimuli, such as visits to the vet hospital and groomer, walks in town, rides on elevators and escalators, sounds of cars, motorcycles, and skateboards, people of different ages, sexes, and ethnicities, people who dress, talk and move in strange ways, people with umbrellas, crutches, and wheelchairs.

If you have ever watched a service dog remain calm and responsive to their handlers' requests in the midst of a noisy, bustling environment you have witnessed proof that such a thorough, positive exposure to the outside world really does result in a more confident and well-adjusted dog, one who will easily accept new stimuli, even without prior exposure to that specific experience.

An Ounce of Prevention

Unfortunately, there are many poorly socialized dogs around us. Many are the result of benevolent neglect—dogs who were never taken anywhere, whose owners didn't anticipate the need for them to be socialized.

The easiest way to avoid this problem, as with most serious dog behavior challenges, is through prevention. While your veterinarian, concerned about diseases, may caution you against exposing your new puppy to the real world, failure to do so can result in a poorly socialized adult dog. And, in the long term, lack of socialization can be a bigger threat to your puppy's well-being than the risk of disease.

The answer to this dilemma is to expose a properly vaccinated young dog to a controlled social environment. Take it to a well-run puppy class, where it can meet lots of different people and lots of healthy puppies. Invite friends of all ages and races over and have them dress up in various "costumes"— odd clothes, hats, umbrellas, sunglasses. Invite children over to play gently and to feed it treats.

The more positive encounters a dog experiences while the socialization window is open—between four and 20 weeks—the more well-adjusted, confident, and gregarious it will be as an adult.

A Pound of Cure

If you're the owner of an unsocialized adult dog, don't despair; steps can be taken to make the world a less terrifying place for these canines. The quality of their lives can be improved with desensitization, and with training that gives them confidence and helps them make sense of the world around them. It takes a lot of work and a patient owner, but it can be done.

The methods used to rehabilitate an unsocialized dog must be positive ones. The poor pooch is already terrified of the world. Progress is slow in the best of circumstances, and once it starts taking tentative steps to emerge from its shell, the tiniest correction can send her scurrying back to safety. Each dog will progress at its own pace. Be patient; pushing an unsocialized dog too quickly can destroy weeks, even months, of painstaking progress.

Encouraging Courage

Teach your dog a bridge, or reward marker. A bridge is a word or a sound that tells your dog that she has earned a reward. The clicker, a small plastic box that makes a clicking sound when pressed, is often used as the bridge in dog training. Your unsocialized dog may be sound sensitive. If so, you may want to start with a one-syllable bridge word, such as "Yes!" instead of the clicker. "Good Dog!" is not a good choice for a reward marker. It's too long. A dog can do several behaviors during the time it takes to say two syllables. Which one is getting rewarded? Besides, we tend to say "Good dog!" to our dogs all the time just because we love them. We need a marker that only means "a reward is coming."

1. To teach your Timid Tess the bridge, just say "Yes!" (or Click! the clicker if she tolerates the sound), and immediately feed her a small but very tasty treat. She doesn't have to do anything special to get the Yes! and treat at first, but do try to avoid marking and treating if she is doing something you don't want her to do, like jumping on you.

If Tess is unsocialized even with you and won't come close enough to eat treats out of your hand, toss the treats to her at a distance or scatter treats all over the ground, and Yes! or Click! every time she picks one up. Once she knows that the marker means "Treat!" you can, for the rest of her life, click! (or yes!) and treat her every time she does something good; this will reinforce that behavior and increase the likelihood that she will do it again.

2. Reward-mark her entire meal. Let this be the only way Tess gets to eat—by being in your company and eventually, when she's brave enough, by eating out of your hand. She needs to learn that you are the source of all good things.

3. Reward-mark her for calm behavior around others. Once Tess knows that the bridge means "Treat!" you can Yes! or Click! and treat anytime she is being brave. If she is normally afraid of children and she sits quietly next to you on a park bench while a child walks by, Yes! and reward. Look for very small, rewardable behaviors. If she glances at a child and doesn't react, Yes! and reward.

4. Make a list of your dog's "fear triggers." You probably have a good idea of what frightens Tess. These are her "fear triggers." Decide which trigger you want to start with in your pooch's desensitization program. Start with something achievable—for your dog's sake and for yours, it's important to have small successes throughout the process. If one is a particularly big trigger, you might have to figure out how to break it down into smaller pieces.

For example: If the Number 1 Trigger is tall men with beards and cowboy hats, you might start with tall, clean-shaven men. Start leaving cowboy hats around the house in conspicuous places, and occasionally put one on yourself. Other family members and people who are well-liked by Tess can do the same. Once she accepts tall men, you can advance to clean-shaven tall men with cowboy hats. Meanwhile, work at desensitizing her to short men with beards. Then try tall men with beards without cowboy hats. When you have desensitized her to all the of the pieces, then you can finally put them together as tall men with beards wearing cowboy hats.

This takes time and patience. If you skip steps, or go too fast, you may undo all of your painstaking training progress and have to start over.

5. Use counter-conditioning and desensitization. Desensitization is the process of gradually acclimating a dog to the things she is afraid of. Counter-conditioning means replacing her undesirable reaction—fear—with a more desirable one that is incompatible with fear, such as the eager anticipation of a tasty treat.

6. Reward-mark while others *feed treats. The ultimate goal is to have Tess believe that people are safe and good, not scary and dangerous. The more she will accept treats from others, the more she can associate them with good things, not just you.*

7. Teach her to target. "Targeting" is teaching your dog to touch a target with her nose on cue. It's easy to do, and it's a great confidence builder for timid dogs.

To start, hold a target object—such as your hand, a pencil, or a short (2-3 foot) dowel—in front of you. Use something that won't frighten her. When she touches it with her nose, Click! or say Yes! and feed her a treat. (If she won't touch it, rub a meaty-flavored treat on it so it smells irresistible.) When she is eagerly touching the target, add the cue-word "Touch!" as she does it. Continue to Click! and treat. In short order she will be eager to touch the target when you ask her to.

Dogs love this exercise. It's like a treat vending machine—push the button, get a treat. By placing the target, which they love, near something they are leery of, you can get them to approach the scary object. When they get clicked and treated for touching the target near the object, they soon decide that the scary thing isn't so bad.

Don't Overprotect!

Tempting as it may be, do not allow yourself to coddle and comfort your Timid Tess. This rewards and reinforces her timid behavior, rather than giving her confidence. If you act concerned, she will be even more convinced that there is something to be afraid of. Instead, act matter-of-fact, jolly her up, and let her know there's nothing wrong. The target stick works really well in place of coddling.

Remember, your unsocialized dog is not acting out of spite or malice. She is truly afraid, even terrified, of the things that she reacts to. Help her to learn—slowly—that the world is not such a frightening place after all. 🐾

15

Jumping Jiminy

Keeping four on the floor is simply a matter of basic training and positive reinforcement.

There are lots of reasons why dogs jump up on people. Jumping up is one of many unacceptable behaviors that can be avoided by starting your pup's training sooner rather than later. Basic training establishes good communication between you and your dog, makes it easier to modify his behavior when you have a specific problem, and cements the bond that is so important to a lifelong relationship.

Mixed Messages

Dogs greet each other by sniffing noses, but when they try to give us a polite canine greeting by jumping up to sniff our faces, we yell, knee them in the chest, smack them on the nose, grab their front paws, squirt lemon juice in their mouths, or stomp on their hind feet.

These are just some of the punitive methods that have been applied in an effort to teach dogs not to jump on humans. **The most effective solution is simple and nonviolent**: Reward the behavior that you want to reinforce, and ignore the behavior that you want to discourage.

Often a dog is rewarded for jumping. When puppies are small, we pick them up and cuddle them, teaching them that "up" is a very nice place to be. When dogs jump, someone usually pets them or pays attention to them, rewarding the very behavior that should be discouraged. Dogs that get rewarded for jumping will just keep doing it.

For some dogs, even the coercive techniques that are meant to be punishments are perceived as rewards—plenty of Labrador Retrievers consider a knee in the chest an invitation to a vigorous game of Body Slam. But how do we ignore jumping? When we simply stand still, Jiminy gets our attention by slapping his paws on our chest.

We have found some effective exercises and management tools for teaching Jumping Jiminy that four-on-the-floor can be much more rewarding than any of his aerial maneuvers.

Consistency is important. Never reward jumping up, and be sure to ask your friends and family members to react appropriately to the dog's antics, too. Behaviors that are rewarded randomly can become very strong—the dog learns that if he just keeps trying, sooner or later, his jump will be rewarded. He will occasionally succeed in jumping on you, but don't encourage him by hugging or petting him when he does.

If you begin these training exercises with a young puppy, you will never have to deal with an adult dog that is leaping and jumping. Adult dogs can be retrained, but the problem is much simpler if the dog never learns the behavior in the first place!

Training Exercises

#1: The on-leash jump with strangers

Hold Jiminy on a leash next to you. Ask a helper to approach the dog and stop just out of leash range, holding a treat against her chest. Hold the leash and stand still. Now, wait.Jiminy will be frustrated that he can't jump on the helper and will sit down to ponder his dilemma. As soon as he sits, ask the helper to say "Yes!" and pop the treat in the dog's mouth. Relax the tension on the leash so the dog is holding the sit himself and is not being restrained.

After about six repetitions, Jiminy will start to sit as the helper approaches. If he tries to leap up to get the treat when it's offered, have the helper whisk it out of reach and say in a cheerful voice, "Too bad, Jiminy!" When the dog sits again, the helper should say "Yes!" and offer the treat. Jiminy will soon learn that he'll get the treat by sitting tight, not by jumping.

If you prefer, you can say "Yes!" and pop the treat in the dog's mouth. This way, he'll learn to look at you and sit as people approach, instead of looking at the people. Repeat this exercise with as many different helpers as possible. Jiminy will learn quickly to sit instead of jump when strangers approach.

#2: The on-leash jump with you

You may not always have a helper handy, so here's a training exercise you can practice on your own. Attach Jiminy's leash to a solid object (if he chews on his leash, use a tie-down—a plastic-coated cable with snaps at both ends).

Walk about 30 feet away, then turn around and start walking back to your dog. As long as he remains seated, keep approaching. The instant he jumps up, stop walking. When he sits, move forward again.

In this exercise, the dog's reward for sitting is simply that you come closer. Give Jiminy a food treat if he is still sitting when you reach him, but you don't have to toss him one every time he sits. Try turning your back on him or backing up a step when he stands, which may encourage him to sit even sooner.

IF YOU BEGIN THESE TRAINING EXERCISES WITH A YOUNG PUPPY, YOU WILL NEVER HAVE TO DEAL WITH AN ADULT DOG THAT IS LEAPING AND JUMPING.

#3: The off-leash jump

Jiminy flies over the sofa to greet you when you get home. You know exactly what's coming. There's no leash to restrain him. What should you do?

This is simple... *Turn your back on him.* Watch him out of the corner of your eye, and turn and step away as he tries to jump. If you consistently repeat this behavior, Jiminy will eventually sit in frustration. The instant he sits, say "Yes!" in a bright voice, feed him a treat, and pet him (if he enjoys being petted; not all dogs do).

For this exercise, you have to have a treat with you when you walk in the door. I suggest you keep a jar of biscuits on the front stoop—or carry cookies in your pockets all the time. If the dog starts to jump again after eating the treat, turn and step away. Repeat this response until he realizes that sitting—not jumping—gets him the attention he's looking for.

To avoid reinforcing the wrong behavior, be sure to give the "Yes" marker only when the dog is sitting, not before. "Yes!" means "Whatever behavior you are doing at the instant that you hear this word has earned you a treat."

Sometimes, a series of behaviors can become connected or "chained" together because the dog thinks the reward follows the performance of all the behaviors, not just the last one.

For example, Jiminy might learn the short behavior chain of "jump up, sit, get reward." To avoid confusion, frequently reward the dog whenever he sits without jumping. He will soon learn exactly which behavior earns the reward.

Time Out

When Jiminy is out of control and jumping on the company (or you!), deliver a cheerful, "Too bad, Jiminy, time out!" and have him spend a few minutes on his tie-down.

A tie-down is a plastic-coated cable, about 4 to 6 feet long, with snaps on both ends. You can secure one end to a heavy piece of furniture or attach it to an eye bolt. Place a comfortable rug or bed nearby.

If you know in advance that Jiminy is going to maul Aunt Maude the instant she walks in the door, clip him to the tie-down before you open the door.

Release him when he settles down. If, after you release him, he revs up again, repeat the message: "Too bad, Jiminy, time out!"

Remember, despite your frustration, your tone should be cheerful, not punishing or forceful. The dog will gradually learn to control his own behavior in order to avoid time-outs, and you won't need to yell at him at all to get him to stay on all fours.

#4: Asking for alternate behavior

When Jiminy approaches, ask for him to sit or lie down before he has a chance to jump. Reward the behavior with a "Yes!" and a treat. After several repetitions, the dog may offer those behaviors before you even ask.

This exercise only works if your dog responds well to the verbal cues "Sit" and "Down." If he does not, and you have to repeat the cues several times—with Jiminy jumping up on you all the while—you are actually rewarding the dog (with your attention) for bad behavior. The dog is also learning to ignore your verbal cues for sitting and lying down.

#5: Jumping on cue

This exercise is only recommended if you find a dog's antics endearing and want to encourage him to jump *occasionally*. If so, teach the dog a verbal cue for jumping—and that the only time it's okay to jump is when someone gives that cue.

Reward the dog for jumping only after he has been invited to jump. Don't pat your chest or include any other gesture when giving the cue, because strangers and children may unknowingly repeat the gesture and signal the dog to jump.

Jumping is a normal, natural behavior for dogs. It is the owner's responsibility to communicate that jumping up-like so many other normal dog behaviors-is unacceptable in human society. Help make Jiminy a more welcome member of the human pack by training and rewarding acceptable replacement behaviors. If you start early, it's easier than you think!

16

Your Dog and the Law

Just as motorists can be held liable for damage they do with their cars, dog owners can be held liable for harm done by their dogs.

Dogs and people have lived in relative harmony for thousands of years. But as population growth brings both species physically closer, an ever-growing body of "dog law" is emerging intended to strengthen, not threaten, the institution of dog ownership. They safeguard an individual's right to own a dog while also assuring the public's health and safety.

"Think of dog-related laws as opportunities to protect the public, yourself, and your dog," advises Jerrold Tannenbaum, an attorney, ethicist, and clinical associate professor of environmental studies at Tufts University School of Veterinary Medicine. Knowing—and abiding by—your state and local dog laws will help you avoid disputes with neighbors and unpleasant encounters with the legal system.

Dogs as Property

Legally speaking, pet dogs are domestic animals. As such, the law considers them the property of their owners. (Wild animals, on the other hand, are technically the property of the state, unless the state gives private citizens permission to own them.) But the law attaches certain conditions and obligations to the privilege of owning a dog, just as it does to the privilege of owning and driving a car. Just as motorists can be held liable for damage they do with their cars, dog owners can be held liable for harm done by their dogs.

Liability

Your state's liability law for damage or injury caused by dogs can rely on two quite different tests: negligence (the failure to act as a reasonable and prudent person would act under the given circumstances) and strict liability (automatic liability regardless of fault). In all states, negligent owners can be held liable for harm done by their dogs. And a growing number of states impose strict liability on owners for dog-related injury and damage.

No matter which state criterion applies, your local government probably wields a good deal of authority over animal-control issues. Although the Constitution prohibits the government from seizing property (including dogs) without due process (notification and the opportunity to be heard), Tannenbaum says, "States and localities have enormous leeway in determining exactly what the notice and the opportunity to be heard will be." Consequently, many dogs suffer impoundment (capture and confinement) while people untangle the legal knots.

As the name implies, strict liability is the most stringent form of liability. Strict-liability laws dictate that an owner is liable for injury (and, in some states, damage) caused by his or her dog regardless of whether the owner is negligent. Some strict-liability statutes, however, do not impose liability for dog-caused injury to trespassers or to anyone who has taunted or provoked the animal. But because mail carriers and delivery people have an "implied invitation" to be on your premises, technically they are not trespassing, so you'll incur liability if your dog bites such a person. Also, most states do not view a child who wanders uninvited onto your property as a trespasser. So if your dog bites such a child, you'll probably be held liable.

The rule of negligence says that owners are responsible for injury or damage if they knew, or if a reasonable person should have known, that the dog would do harm under the given circumstances. Some mistakenly call this the "one-bite" rule, thinking—incorrectly—that the law gives each dog owner one "free bite." The one-bite fallacy is based on the discredited theory that an owner cannot possibly know that a dog is dangerous until it has actually bitten someone. (In fact, a dog's growling or teeth baring could be a precursor to more harmful forms of aggression and should put the owner on notice.)

To understand the difference between the two liability theories, consider this scenario: your friend, who has known and played with your always affectionate pooch for years, is visiting at your invitation. Without warning, the dog bites your friend's leg. Under strict liability, you are liable even though you had no reason to know your dog might bite and therefore no reason to take precautions.

On the other hand, under the negligence rule, you would not be legally responsible for failing to protect your friend. You did not know—nor could you have known—that the dog would bite, and therefore, you would not be found negligent. (Common courtesy, however, might impel you to reimburse your friend's medical expenses.)

Note also that in some jurisdictions, anyone harboring a dog is considered legally responsible for damage done by the dog. And if you care for a stray (an apparently unowned dog), you might be responsible for the consequences of the dog's behavior while it is under your care, even if the legal owner eventually turns up.

DOG OWNERS SHOULD HAVE SUFFICIENT LIABILITY COVERAGE TO TAKE CARE OF ANY CONCEIVABLE DAMAGE...

Insurance To The Rescue?

The good news is that, should Bowser trample the Jeffersons' prized petunias, your homeowner's or renter's insurance policy probably covers dog-created damage, regardless of fault. Review your insurance policy, and call your agent if the legal jargon confuses you. Most homeowner's policies offer liability coverage from $100,000 to $300,000. "Dog owners should have sufficient liability coverage to take care of any conceivable damage," advises Tannenbaum.

The not-so-good news is that many insurance companies invoke their own "one-bite" rule. After the first dog-bite claim, they may cancel the insurance or exclude dog-related incidents from the coverage. Owners of "problem" dogs may therefore have to pay high rates to specialty insurance companies to cover dog liability.

Even with insurance protection, you're still better off spending the time to raise a well-mannered dog than winding up in a legal dispute because you've ignored the basics of good canine citizenship. Visit your town hall or contact a local dog club to learn what's on the books about dogs. Find out if your state applies strict liability or less stringent criteria.

Licensing & Vaccinations

Most states and local governments require licensing of dogs. License records help reunite lost dogs with their owners—which only works if your dog wears its license tag. Most courts have ruled that if a dog is unlicensed (as untagged dogs often are assumed to be) and running at large (roaming freely and not under a person's control), the local government has the power to impound the dog.

Licensing also helps the state keep track of vaccination histories. Almost all states require vaccination of dogs older than 4 to 6 months. Most cities and towns require proof of rabies vaccination before they will license your dog. Some cities also require proof of distemper vaccination. But these are only minimum legal requirements. Your veterinarian may recommend further vaccination protection Also, because vaccination laws vary from state to state, it's wise to carry vaccination records when traveling with your dog.

Canine Good Citizenship

Dog-related legal problems usually arise because owners fail to adequately restrain or train their dogs. Here's how to avoid run-ins with your neighbors or local officials:

■ *Never let your dog run at large.*

■ *Keep your dog's license and vaccinations current.*

■ *Closely supervise your dog among strangers and children—both on and off your property.*

■ *Train your dog in basic obedience and quickly remedy behavioral problems.*

■ *Curb excessive barking. If your dog interferes with the neighbors' enjoyment of their property, you could find yourself facing a nuisance complaint.*

Leash Laws

Most densely populated municipalities have dog-restraint laws. The language of these laws varies, but they generally require that a dog be on a leash and under control when not on the owner's premises. In most leash-law-governed communities, animal-control officials can automatically impound dogs running at large—even if they are licensed and tagged. In rural areas of several states, animal-control officials (and, sometimes, landowners) can legally kill your dog if they catch it attacking or "worrying" livestock. Therefore, dog owners living anywhere near livestock should never let their dogs run loose.

If your town has a leash law and your dog damages property or causes personal injury while at large, the law will probably consider you automatically negligent and therefore responsible for making restitution. Even if your community does not have a leash law, you may still be held liable under state law for damage or injury your dog causes.

Public Health

Some cities, concerned about health risks posed by large concentrations of dogs, limit the number of dogs per household. Despite challenges to such laws, Tannenbaum says that "the courts have been virtually unanimous in ruling that the government has the right to protect the public peace, health, and safety by enacting such laws."

As some people have learned the hard way, urban and suburban dogs often have no choice but to "do their business" in public. In response, many heavily populated communities have passed so-called "pooper-scooper" laws as a public-health measure. Even the most ardent dog lover who has stepped in publicly deposited dog droppings appreciates the value of these ordinances.

Handling Disputes

What can you do if the dog whose barking is driving you insane is not your dog? Probably the most common complaint about dogs is the noise they make. The good news for neighbors is that usually problems can be resolved without resorting to legal means, through informal negotiation or mediation. And if that fails, there is almost always a law against noisy nuisance dogs.

If you canít get these laws enforced to your satisfaction, you can sue the dog owner to get the nuisance stopped and to recover money damages. But substituting a major hassle with expensive lawyers for a small one with a bad-mannered spaniel isn't much progress. Lawsuits are especially undesirable when the other party is a neighbor — after all, you'll still be next door to each other no matter who wins.

Here are some ways to resolve neighborhood dog disputes out of court and stay on relatively good terms with the neighbors.

Talking to your neighbor

The obvious first step — asking the dog's owner to stop the noise — is either ignored or botched by a surprising number of people, probably because approaching someone with a complaint can be unpleasant and even intimidating.

However, talking to your neighbor calmly and reasonably is an essential first step. Even if you do eventually end up in court, a judge isn't likely to be too sympathetic if you didn't make at least some effort to work things out first. So it's a no-lose situation, and if you approach it with a modicum of tact, you may be pleasantly surprised.

Sometimes owners are blissfully unaware that there's a problem. If a dog barks for hours every day — but only when it's left alone — the owner may not know that a neighbor is being driven crazy by a dog the owner thinks is quiet and well-mannered. Even if you're sure the neighbor does know about the dog's antisocial behavior, it may be better to proceed as though she doesn't.

Getting the Most From Negotiations

■ *Write a friendly note or call to arrange a convenient time to talk. Don't blunder up some rainy evening when the neighbor is trying to drag groceries and kids in the house after work.*

■ *If you think it's appropriate, take a little something to the meeting to break the ice: some vegetables from your garden, perhaps.*

■ *Don't threaten legal action (or worse, illegal action). There will be time to discuss legal remedies if relations deteriorate.*

■ *Offer positive suggestions. Once you have established some rapport, you may want to suggest, tactfully, that the owner get help with the dog. Try saying something like, "You know, my friend Tom had the same problem with his dog, and since he's been taking the dog to ABC Obedience School classes, he and his neighbors are much happier." Of course, if you make suggestions too early in the process, the neighbor may resent your "interference."*

■ *Try to agree on specific actions to alleviate the problem: for example, that the dog is kept inside between 10 p.m. and 8 a.m.*

■ *After you agree on a plan, set a date to talk again in a couple of weeks. If your next meeting is already arranged, it will be easier for you to talk again. It won't look like you're badgering your neighbor, but will show that you're serious about getting the problem solved.*

■ *If the situation improves, make a point to say thanks. Not only is it the nice thing to do, it will also encourage more progress.*

Mediation: Getting another person to help

If talking to your neighbor directly doesn't work, or you're convinced it's hopeless, consider getting some help from a mediator. A mediator won't make a decision for you, but will help you and your neighbor agree on a resolution of the problem.

Mediators, both professional and volunteers, are trained to listen to both sides, identify problems, keep everyone focused on the real problems and suggest compromises. Going through the process helps both people feel they've been heard (a more constructive version of the satisfaction of "having your day in court") and often puts people on better terms.

Mediation provides a safe, structured way for neighbors to talk. They meet informally with one or more mediators, and first agree on ground rules—basic guidelines, such as no name-calling or interrupting. Then, each person briefly states a view of the problem. The mediator may summarize the problem and its history before moving on to discuss possible solutions.

Unlike a lawsuit, mediation is not an adversarial process. You do not go to mediation to argue your side. No judge-like person makes a decision for you. People can become amazingly cooperative when they realize they are empowered to resolve their own problem.

When two people do agree on how to alleviate the problem, it's best to put the agreement in writing, which helps clarify everyone's expectations. And it's invaluable if later memories grow fuzzy, as they almost always do, about who agreed to do what.

The best place to look for a free mediator for this kind of dispute is a community mediation group. Many cities have such groups, which usually train volunteers to mediate disputes in their neighborhoods. Other places that may be able to refer you to a mediation service include the small claims court clerk's office, the local district attorney's office, radio or television stations that offer help with consumer problems, or state or local bar associations.

Dangerous-Dog Laws

The question of how to deal with dogs that bite or attack is a highly provocative one. So ordinances that stipulate conditions for owning—and punishing—dogs deemed "dangerous" or "vicious" inevitably provoke controversy. Local and state laws banning or severely restricting ownership of specific breeds have incited the most debate.

According to the American Kennel Club (AKC), 165 of the 320 municipalities that have dangerous-dog ordinances target specific breeds. But such laws often fail to assign responsibility where it really lies. "It doesn't make sense to blame the dog for what it has done when the real problem is the owner," says Professor Andrew Rowan, director of the Center for Animals and Public Policy at Tufts University School of Veterinary Medicine. Such laws attribute viciousness to bloodlines alone, ignoring the fact that dogs can learn aggressive behavior from—or have it reinforced by—irresponsible, careless owners. These laws also discriminate against responsible owners of targeted breeds—those who raise upstanding canine citizens by carefully training and properly socializing their dogs.

Moreover, breed-specific ordinances can backfire. Many cities that outlawed or restricted pit bull ownership in the late 1980s saw the population of other potentially pugnacious breeds soar. (And occasionally dogs that merely looked like members of a restricted or banned breed were victimized.) "Breed-specific restrictions don't change the total number of dogs capable of administering a nasty bite," observes Professor Rowan. "All such regulations do is change the local breed distribution." Having realized these shortcomings, 146 communities that once considered or enacted breed-specific ordinances now have more general regulations.

Among the most progressive localities is Multnomah County, Oregon. In 1986, the county enacted an ordinance that strikes the delicate balance between public safety and the rights of responsible dog owners. Multnomah's system, developed by a task force of animal-control personnel, dog club representatives, public health officials, and veterinarians, places offending dogs (regardless of breed)—and their owners—in one of five categories. The more serious the infraction, the stiffer the restrictions, which range from physically confining the dog and requiring the owner to pass a responsible pet-ownership test to euthanizing the dog and suspending the owner's right to keep dogs.

Multnomah's classification scheme works. In the first three years (1986-89), recidivism (the number of repeat biting or attacking incidents) fell from 25 to 7 percent. Consistent enforcement and precise record-keeping also contribute to the system's success. "If Multnomah County-type programs were instituted nationwide, I think the incidence of dog bites—certainly serious dog bites—would drop dramatically," concludes Professor Rowan.

State and local laws

If the situation doesn't improve after your efforts to work something out, it's time to check your local laws and see what your legal options are. Armed with this knowledge, you'll be better prepared to approach your neighbor again or go to animal control authorities, the police or a small claims court.

In some places, barking dogs are covered by a specific state or local ordinance. If there's no law aimed specifically at dogs, a general nuisance or noise ordinance will make the owner responsible. Local law may forbid loud noise after 10 p.m., for example, or prohibit any "unreasonable" noise. And someone who allows a dog to bark, after numerous warnings from police, may be arrested for disturbing the peace.

To find out what the law is where you live, go to a law library and check the state statutes and city or county), ordinances yourself. Look in the index under "noise," "dogs," "animals" or "nuisance." If you don't have access to a law library, you can probably find out about local laws by calling the local animal control agency or city attorney.

Animal control authorities

If your efforts at working something out with your neighbor haven't succeeded, talk to the animal control department in your city or county. The people there are likely to be more receptive than the police or other municipal officials.

When you call, don't just make your complaint and hang up. If it's really a persistent problem, you need to be persistent, too. Ask the person you talk to—and write down his name, so you won't have to explain your problem every time you call—about the department's procedures. Find out what the department will do, and when. For example, the department may need to receive a certain number of complaints about a barking dog within a certain time before it will act.

Some cities have set up special programs to handle dog complaints. The animal control department establishes a simple procedure for making a complaint, and follows up promptly—and repeatedly, if necessary. This is a great idea, for two main reasons. First, it gives a specific city official or department—usually the health, police or public safety department—responsibility for the problem. If it's not clear who's primarily responsible, someone with a complaint is likely to get shuffled from department to department.

Police

The police aren't very interested in barking dog problems, and you can't much blame them. Unless you live in an exceptionally quiet and peaceful place, police have lots more serious problems on their hands than barking dogs.

Another reason to avoid the police, except as a last resort, is that summoning a police cruiser to a neighbor's house obviously will not improve your already strained relations. But if none of the options already discussed works, and the relationship with your neighbor is shot anyway, you might as well give the police a try. The police may be your only choice, too, if you don't know who owns the offending dog, as can happen on crowded city blocks where you just can't tell whose dog is making the noise.

The police have the power to enforce local noise laws and laws that prohibit disturbing the peace. As when you're dealing with animal control people, don't be afraid to ask the police exactly what you and other neighbors must do to get them to take action. You may well have to make more than one call or written complaint.

Small claims court

If nothing you've tried helps, you can sue the owner of a barking dog, on the ground that the dog is a nuisance that interferes with your use and enjoyment of your home. The least painful route is through small claims court. Small claims court procedures are simple and designed to be used without a lawyer. In some states, including California, lawyers are barred from small claims court. Even if they aren't banned, you will rarely see one there because most people find it too expensive to hire them. Fees in small claims court are also low, and the process is relatively fast—which means you'll get to court in a few weeks or months, not years.

Winning a lawsuit in small claims court can get you money (and satisfaction), but probably nothing else. In most states, small claims court judges only have the power to order someone to pay money. They can't give you what you really want—a court order telling your neighbor to make the problematic pooch be quiet.

Still, making your neighbor fork over some money may be even more effective than a simple court order in convincing your neighbor to clean up his (or his dog's) act. And you can keep going back to court and asking for more as long as the nuisance continues.

If you absolutely must have a court order telling the neighbor to stop (the technical term for this kind of order is an injunction), you may have to go to "regular" court (often called circuit, superior or district court) instead of small claims court. For that, you'll probably need a lawyer, though you can bring a straightforward nuisance suit yourself, if you're willing to spend some hours in the law library finding out how to draw up the papers and submit them to the court.

Section IV

Training Tools

17

Proper Crate Training

*Besides offering a quiet refuge,
crates used properly are valuable training tools,
not punishment or prisons.*

Why crates? In the wild, most canines rely on snug, enclosed areas (dens) to bear and raise pups. The den contributes to pack survival and offers protection. It seems that the wild *canis*'s yen for denning "persists in domesticated dogs, and denlike settings have a calming effect," says Fred Harrington, a wolf-behavior expert and professor of psychology at Mt. St. Vincent University in Halifax, Nova Scotia.

Crates (manmade dens) can be remarkably versatile. For a puppy, a warm, snug crate works as a house-training aid (dogs typically won't soil their "personal space"), a temporary playpen when you can't directly supervise the pup, and a cozy bedroom that can comfort the pup during those first few stressful nights away from littermates.

Crates are, hands down, the safest way for dogs to travel in cars; they are "musts" for canine air travel; and they are a "home away from home" in hotels where pets are allowed. They offer quiet refuge when a dog is recuperating from an illness or injury and can be a sanctuary when things get hectic around the house. "Every dog should have a place to call its own," notes Dr. Nicholas Dodman, director of the Behavior Clinic at Tufts University School of Veterinary Medicine.

As long as they're not used for punishment, crates can also help correct undesirable canine behaviors—such as destructive chewing. More important, crates can help prevent behavior problems before they start by helping owners establish routines for their dogs.

They can be used to help dogs teach themselves two very impotant skills: The first is eliminating only when and where it is appropriate; the second is keeping out of trouble—behaving appropriately in the house. Without these two skills, a dog doesn't have much of a chance in this world.

What Are Crates For?

Potty training

The first proper use of a crate is to teach a puppy or dog to eliminate only when and where it is appropriate.

You can teach this to an adult dog within three days. using the "umbilical cord" method: The dog is tied to your waist so you can watch it every second.

Then, every hour on the hour you take it outside, to the place where you want it to eliminate. When they do, you give them three treats, take them back inside, and let them off the leash for a little while.

If they do not eliminate, they do not get a treat, and they go back inside still on the leash. By the fourth day, there usually are no more mistakes.

Puppies may or may not take a little longer to potty-train. Your consistency will make all the difference. When at home, confine the puppy whenever you cannot watch it every minute. Few dogs or puppies will soil their bedrooms unless they are really desperate; but don't keep the puppy,or any dog, for that matter, in there long enough to get desperate.

Every hour on the hour, release the puppy, saying, "Let's go potty!" and run with it to its doggie toilet. (Running is helpful because you don't want an accident to happen on the way to the toilet, and because running jiggles the puppy's bladder and bowels.)

Most puppies will urinate within two minutes. If it does, reward it with three liver treats, and go back in the house. By doing this, you actually instill in the puppy the desire to wait until you come home and take it outside to eliminate—because that's the only time it can cash in its urine and feces for treats!

Once the puppy has eliminated, take it back into the house and turn it loose, wherever it can spend some time exploring under supervision. Then you only have to make sure it doesn't chew the wrong things! After an hour or so, put it back into the crate, and start the process again. However, if your puppy doesn't eliminate, it has to go back in the crate for another hour, and you start the procedure all over again.

Housetraining

Potty-training is what most people are worried about, of course, but house-training is just as important, and, fortunately, it's a nice side-effect of crate-training.

In just a matter of days, the dog will learn that every time he is confined, he gets to chew on toys, and soon, he'll become addicted to chewing toys. That means he won't destroy the rest of your house, and it mean he won't become a recreational barker. He'll still alert you when the doorbell rings, but recreational chewers almost never become annoying chronic barkers.

The dog will also self-train itself to settle down and enjoy time spent at home alone. After a week or two of this procedure, the adult dog can safely enjoy the full run of his home for the rest of his life. Again, it's not advised that puppies be left alone for any length of time until they are at least 12 months old.

What Are Crates NOT For

Crates are perhaps second only to choke collars as the most mis-used training equipment forced upon dogs. However, unlike choke collars, there is a terrific training principle behind the use of crates.They are not for punishing your dog for doing something wrong; if used in this way, the dog will quickly learn to avoid ever going in

If you do your job properly, your dog will regard his crate as his favorite place to lie down and relax or sleep.

the crate, or how to be as obnoxious as possible in order to get let out.

Nor are they for "warehousing" a number of dogs, so you don't have too many underfoot. Breeders abuse the use of crates more than all other dog owners. You often see breeders who don't actually want to live with the dogs they breed and raise; they use crates to contain their merchandise, until it's ready to sell. This is in itself objectionable, but even more so when this prison concept is forced upon the people who buy their dogs and puppies. Many people faithfully lock their perfectly well-behaved dogs in crates for hours every day because the breeder they bought the dog from told them they had to. Simply stated, crates are not for long-term close confinement of puppies *or* adult dogs. They are too small; any animal suffers when it is forced to stay that closely confined for more than a few hours.

Puppies Are Babies

Crates are also not for keeping puppies out of trouble all day. Puppies are just like babies; they need to be watched every minute, and few puppy owners seem to understand this. People make arrangements for their new babies to be supervised when they are away from home; they have to learn to do the same with puppies.

When the puppy gets older, say, six to 12 months old, you can begin leaving it for longer periods of time. However, you can't just go out the door and hope for the best. You have to teach your puppy how to cope with short-term close confinement, and later, with long-term confinement.

Long-term Confinement

Until your new dog is house-trained, you can't give it the run of the house all day while you are at work—but you can't leave it in the crate, either—it's too small. Instead, when you're away from home, use long-term confinement to keep your dog out of trouble.

The most suitable place for teaching long-term confinement would be a bathroom, one with all the toilet paper, towels, shower curtains, and carpets removed. Leave only a few things in there: the dog's bed, an adequate supply of water, some safe hollow chew toys which are stuffed with food treats, and the dog's toilet. For the latter, something like two short rolls of turf on a sheet of plastic would do. The benefit of this, rather than those commercial puppy pads, is that the dog will train itself to urinate on turf or dirt.

If your new dog is extremely anxious, and takes desperate measures to escape, such as tearing the bathroom door apart, you can't use this method. You will need to consult a professional for advice on dealing with extreme separation anxiety.

The long-term confinement method is a temporary measure, only meant to keep your new dog out of trouble until you have the time to potty- and house-train it.

A PUPPY SHOULD REGARD THE CRATE AS HIS PLAYROOM, HIS DOGGY DEN...ON A PAR WITH CONFINING YOUR CHILD TO A ROOM WITH A TV AND VCR, A SEGA, AND A TON OF TOYS.

Crate-training Mistakes

The most common mistake people make with their crates is using it as a prison, or shoving the dog into the crate when he's been bad. That's the very best way to teach your dog to avoid going into the crate at any time.

Instead, a dog should regard the crate as his play room, his doggie den. Confining a dog or puppy to a crate should be on par with confining your child to a room with a TV and VCR, a Sega, and a ton of toys.

This is a simple thing to teach puppies. When a puppy is tired and hungry, you put him in the crate along with his dinner and some toys, and you leave him there. He'll eat his dinner and fall asleep.

If someone has taught an adult dog to have apprehensions about the crate, though, it will probably take at least a few days to overcome them. The process here will be a little different; he ll need additional time to get over his anxiety that he will be locked and trapped in the crate. While you are trying to convince him of this, don t lock and trap him in the crate!

Training Theory

The point of training is to make the dog want to do what *you* want it to do. How can you make a dog want to be in the crate? Food!

First, always feed this dog in his crate, and make the most of his daily ration by feeding it to him in numerous courses—as many as a dozen, even. Put a little food in the crate, let him go in and eat it, and then let him out right after he's finished. Make the final course of the day a big one, mixing his kibble with some juicy canned food. Put the bowl in the crate and then shut the door, with the dog on the outside, and let the dog think about this for a while. After a minute, he'll be saying, "Hey! Open the crate door! Let me in!" This is what training is all about. When your dog is pleading to get in its crate, let it in!

Here's another tactic: Throw a bit of kibble in the crate. Let him go in and get it; he'll come right out again. Do this three or four times. Then, throw a bit of kibble in, and when he goes in to get it, shut the door and immediately feed him another couple of bits of kibble through the bars. Then, let him out, and ignore him for three minutes. Then, put a bit of kibble in the crate, shut the door, feed him five bits of kibble through the bars, and then let him out and ignore him for five minutes.

The next time, put a bunch of kibble in a Kong toy, along with some freeze-dried liver and a bit of honey so it is difficult to get the food out, and put the Kong in the crate. Let the dog in and shut the door. Before he's finished trying to get all the food out, after about 10 minutes, open the door, let him out, take the Kong away, and ignore him for five minutes.

What is the dog learning? That when he's in the crate, his owner talks to him all the time, sits next to him and reads him a book, and keeps feeding him. And there are toys in the crate. There are no toys anywhere else—that crate is OK!

Every dog develops favorite places to lie down. If you've crate-trained your dog properly, that favorite place will be in the crate with the door open. If the dog goes there of his own accord, it's a good sign that you have done a good job as a trainer.

Crate-training Tips

■ *Open-Door Policy: Leave the crate door open until your dog willingly enters and exits on its own. "Dens don't have doors," notes Dr. Dodman.*

- *Activity Alley: Hide food treats in a t-shirt with your smell on it in the crate. The dog will associate the crate with stimulating hide-and-seek activities and the security of your "alpha dog" scent.*
- *Doggie Diner: Feed your dog in its crate so it identifies the "den" with the ultimate canine joy—eating..*
- *Snooze City: Encourage your dog to nap in its crate so it associates the crate with "R & R."*
- *Play Place: Praise, play with, and pet your dog when it's inside the crate..*
- *Snuggle Space: Equip the crate with a warm, soft pad or blanket.*

Crate Criteria

Most crates are made of thick-gauge metal wire or molded plastic. Drs. Dodman and Fetko prefer the plastic crates because their solid walls provide more privacy and security than the "transparent" wire crates. (You can "wall in" a wire crate by throwing a blanket over the sides and back of it.) Whichever material you choose, your dog's crate should be ruggedly constructed and fitted with secure door latches. For portability, look for crates that disassemble or fold up easily.

Above all, make sure your dog's crate is the appropriate size—at least large enough for your dog to stand up, turn around, and lie down in. But a crate shouldn't be too big—especially for a pup. "Young dogs often find spacious quarters more disturbing than comforting," notes Dr. Dodman. Also, a crate that's too large can sabotage house-training because the pup can eliminate at one end and then move to "higher ground." If you're raising a pup, purchase a crate that will be big enough to accommodate it when it's full grown, then insert partitions or cardboard boxes inside the crate to reduce the interior space for the time being.

18

Collars & Leads

The collar you pick has a big—and lasting— effect on training and obedience. Choose wisely from the many available.

There's a great temptation—especially if you live in the country, although city dwellers are guilty of this as well—to let your pet go *au naturel*—without a collar. Don't! Your dog's collar and leash are important tools for training and restraining.

Some owners believe even simple buckle collars can get snagged and choke a dog to death. Although possible, it's highly unlikely. The likelihood of problems and dangers for collarless dogs is far greater. One of the dangers might even be the local dogcatcher. If your dog has no identification on him it could be a painful—even deadly—experience for him.

It's best to get your dog accustomed to wearing a collar as soon as possible. Regardless of whether he's a pup or older, he'll probably resist at first. It's a good idea to let him sniff it at first, but don't let him chew it. If you have a pup, an inexpensive lightweight buckle collar will do the trick. Even with growth holes he'll soon outgrow it, so you don't need to spend a great deal on it. A $5 to $10 nylon fabric or leather buckle collar will do just fine. The collar should fit comfortably,

not too loose or too tight. If it's too tight, he'll choke as he grows; too loose and he'll easily paw or scratch at it and slip out.

Training Collars

When you're ready to train your dog, you'll need to decide what collar is best and most effective for your dog and you. If you believe in the confrontational/aversive conditioning methods of training, you'll probably go to a choke or prong collar.

However, there's a growing movement towards more positive training, which we strongly support. Dr. Nicholas Dodman, director of the Tufts Behavior clinic, believes that almost all dogs can and should be trained through positive reinforcement rather than inflicting pain. "Confrontational techniques, which grew out of World War II methods for training military animals, are outmoded and should be replaced by more motivational methods such as clicker and head-halter training," he said.

Whichever collar you choose for your dog, make sure the hardware on both the collar and leash is sturdy and over time is not wearing out. Fatigue of the metal and material can happen and by checking your equipment frequently many dangerous escapes can be eliminated.

Consider a halter-type collar even for a pup. Proponents of positive dog training highly recommend them and since your dog is going to wiggle and squirm regardless of the style of collar, you may want to consider adapting him to one as a pup. They do cost more than a simple buckle collar— expect to pay anywhere from $10 to $50—and they require more adjustment.

Years ago, dogs were trained most often on chain slip-collars known as chokers. Today, the choices are much wider. The chain collar has been joined by a nylon version, snap-on slip collars, humane chokers, prong collars, head or halter collars and remote or "shock" collars. Each training device has its followers—and some have strong opponents.

The simplest training collar is a **buckle collar**. The most common is the chain-slip collar or **"choke" collar**. Rising in popularity is the prong or **pinch collar**, a torturous-looking device that can be quite effective on boisterous dogs. More appropriate in our view is the halter or **head collar**, which fits the dog's whole head and uses the handler's ability to turn the dog's head rather than neck pressure as the control. Which collar is best for you will depend a great deal on your dog's temperament. Whether he's submissive, dominant, or aggressive will be a key determinant for which type of collar to use.

Types of Collars

Buckle Collars

This is simply a loop of leather or nylon designed like a pants belt. They usually have expansion holes to accommodate growth. Although these can be found for between $5 and $10, you can go as elaborate as you like, with colors, fabrics, designs, glow-in-the-dark and even bells (no whistles). These collars are very, very uncontroversial. They're excellent everyday collars and inexpensive enough to replace frequently for a "new look." For training purposes, if you have a bright, eager-to-please pet, light tugs on these collars may be sufficient. Few of us are that lucky however. With a buckle collar it is next to impossible to correct your dog if you favor physical correction. If you are using food rewards or clicker training methods, such a collar or a head halter will be all you'll ever need.

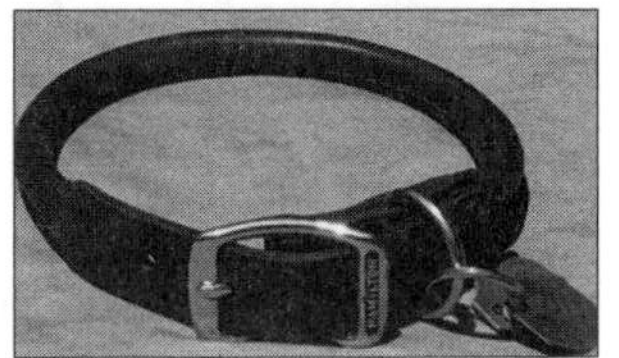

Chokers or Slip-Collars

Slip collars come in either metal or nylon. Metal slips more easily than nylon and can rub fur off the underside of the dog's neck more easily. The portion of the collar that rides on the top of the neck has a ring to which you attach the leash. The chain goes through the ring that is attached to the portion of the collar that goes under the neck.

When purchasing a metal choke collar, you should ensure that the collar is smooth and free slipping. Choke collars work by tightening and loosening a noose around the dog's neck. Despite the name the idea is not to choke your dog. Instead, the premise behind these collars is that when a correction is warranted, a quick jerk and release will convince your dog to see things your way.

Choke collars should fit just below the dog's ears for the best results because this delivers the sharpest correction. Do not use these collars in toy

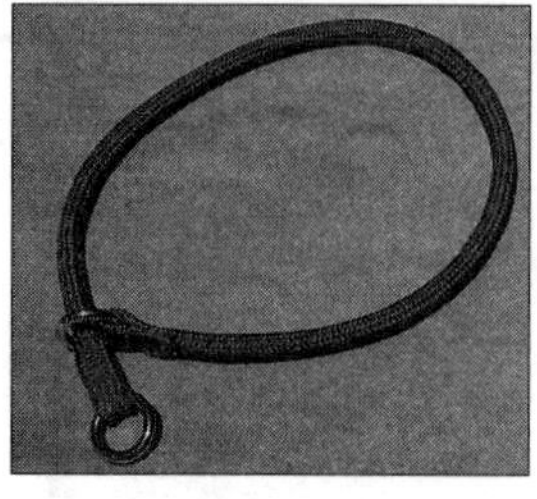

breeds. They are simply too dangerous for tiny dogs. Do not use them if you have to drag your dog along. Know that a hard jerk with a slip collar can damage a dog's trachea or even the spine in the neck region.

"Slip" collars are less effective in dogs with thick necks or thick coats, particularly if they slide out of position, because the physical discomfort they deliver under these circumstances is not as harsh.

Clip-On Nylon Training Collars

Developed by the Volhards, well-known dog trainers and behaviorists, these take the form of a nylon slip collar made of strong, lightweight nylon that has a snap on one end, a floating ring, and a dead ring. Clip-on nylon collars are used like slip collars; the difference is that they come with a metal clip that prevents them from slipping down onto the dog's neck. The clip also eliminates the need to slip the collar over the dog's head.

This style collar offers great control because the collar stays right behind the ears, rather than on the heavily muscled neck area where collars generally ride. These collars tend to be stronger than chain chokers.

Prong Collar

Also called pinch collars, these have interlocking steel links, each with two blunt prongs that pinch the dog's skin when the collar is tightened. Sometimes the collars are put into a cloth tube (like a hair scrunchy). Although they look like medieval torture devices, prong collars are popular tools among many trainers. However, we do not favor them because we do not agree with the principle of using pain to train. Like the choker, this collar is used in a jerk and release manner. However, the owner can deliver a sharper punishment with less effort as compared to a choke collar.

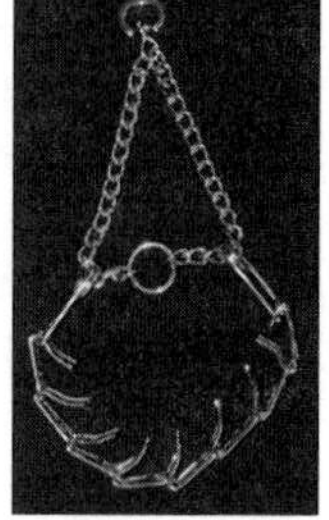

The prong should not be used for aggressive dogs and is too harsh for extremely shy or fearful dogs. Also, *it is not appropriate for young puppies.* **The question is: Should it be used at all?** Says Dr. Dodman, "If you train a dog with positive methods, you'll never need such a device."

Humane Choker

The "humane" choker looks like a prong collar made of chain instead of interlocking links. It has two loops, one of which fits around the dog's neck. The second loop is attached to the first and is used to tighten the chain when necessary to guide the dog or correct his behavior. This collar is becoming more popular among trainers who prefer to teach the dog through motivation rather than correction, which fits right in with the positive reinforcement preferred method of training.

Shock Or Remote Collar

These are easily the most controversial and expensive collars. They consist of two parts: A transmitter which the owner or trainer has, and a receiver that emits a minor shock to a buckle-type collar on the dog. Manufacturers like to call them by the marketing-savvy description "remote collars," while critics prefer the word "shock" or "E" for electric.

These collars have been around since the late 1950s. In the early days of electric collars, they were used mostly as "no" collars by hunters and hikers who liked to let their dogs roam while still exercising control over their activities. Today, they're more often used as training tools.

The major change that facilitated this possible is the current availability of multi-levels of stimulation to work with as opposed to only one excruciatingly painful level in earlier days. Experts who recommend these collars (often grudgingly) say to use them only on the most stubborn dogs. They recommend starting with the mildest shock (equivalent to getting a static shock by walking across a carpet and touching something), and working up to a stronger strength—only if necessary.

However, we believe that using shock for correction is simply wrong and unnecessary. It is too easy to use these collars inappropriately, without the trainer being aware, and they can be can be sadistically abusive in the wrong hands.

The Shocking Truth

The Association of Pet Behaviour Counsellors (APBC) in England issued the following statement:

"The Association of Pet Behaviour Counsellors condemns the widespread use of devices that deliver electric shocks to dogs for the purpose of training or curing behaviour problems. Their potential for accidental misuse is high and they could easily cause considerable and unnecessary pain and distress to the animal.

A dog experiencing an unpleasant shock to the neck 'out of the blue' will associate the sensation with whatever the dog happens to be focusing on at the time. Used incorrectly, this could be an area, object, another dog, the owner or even a child. Unwanted side effects could easily occur when the dog being shocked becomes afraid of being in that area, or it could become afraid of, and as a result, potentially aggressive towards owners, children, other dogs or strangers.

In inexperienced hands, it may take many repetitions of administrations of the shock before the punishment is finally associated with the unwanted behavior, and several more before the dog learns how to avoid the shock by performing the 'correct' action.

Not only is this inhumane, but can set up a series of fears which can cause associated behavior problems in the future. In addition, it is possible that the device may be triggered by external influences, or malfunction, which may result in delivery of repeated shocks, particularly in those devices which are designed to be triggered by barking and are put onto dogs left alone for long periods.

Only in a handful of cases, where all else has been tried and failed, and when the condition is potentially life-threatening, can the use of such devices ever be justified, and, only then, in the hands of an experienced behavioral specialist who is capable of accurate timing."

Head Collar Or Harness

Head halters work by squeezing the dog's muzzle and pressuring the nape of the neck. They are also known as head harnesses and no-pull halters.

A harness is designed to distribute tension over a greater area of the dog's body, which is why they're the best choice for dogs that have injured tracheas or cervical areas and in toy breeds. The head collar or halter has two basic parts; the collar that fits snugly around the dog's neck just in back of his ears, and the face loop that fits loosely over his muzzle and allows complete and gentle control of the head.

The face loop is not a muzzle. The dog can breathe, pant, eat, drink, and kiss your face while wearing the face loop. The leash is attached to the head collar underneath the dog's snoot.

A self-correcting head halter is an effective alternative to more punitive training collars. If your dog charges ahead of you, the leash tightens, the halter directs the dog's head and shoulders back toward you, and the rest of the body follows.

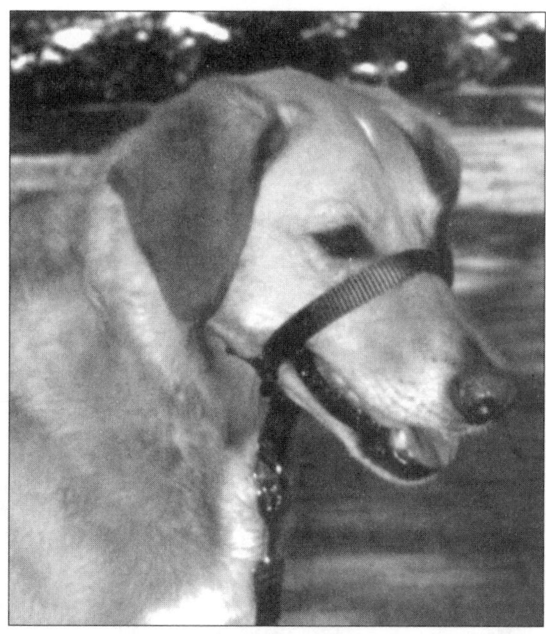

Most dogs fight the head collar at first, but if fitted correctly, the dog will quickly become use to it. To help him adjust, you may want to give him treats when he walks without pawing at the face loop, and calmly control the dog if he tries to remove the loop.

Since the leash is attached to the head collar, gentle pressure upward on the leash will stop the dog from pawing at the loop. If he drops his head to paw at the loop, just lift up and keep walking. If the dog does forge ahead, steady pressure on the leash will turn him back towards you.

■ Headcollars simply do a better job of stopping a pushy puller than all the other types of products on the market—all of them work well to keep the dog from pulling.

■ Headcollars work because they lead the dog from the head, where they lack the strength and leverage to be able to pull. A dog who tries to pull while wearing a headcollar simply has his head turned gently back toward his handler.

Although some high-strung dogs never learn to tolerate wearing something on their head and face, and some need a period of adjustment before they accept them, headcollars are the most effective and humane no-pull aid for most dogs. See *Headcollars* chapter.

Body Harnesses

These are often used on draft dogs to facilitate pulling sleds or carts. They're also used to signal police and guide dogs that it's time for work. Harnesses encourage a dog to move in front of its handler, which is useful for working dogs but counterproductive for casual strolls in the park. The principle: When the dog pulls on the leash, the harness tightens around the dog, causing a low level of discomfort. When the dog stops pulling, the discomfort stops, so the dog is rewarded for not pulling. We asked a consulting trainer to evaluate two brands of no-pull harnesses, below.

Holt Control Harness

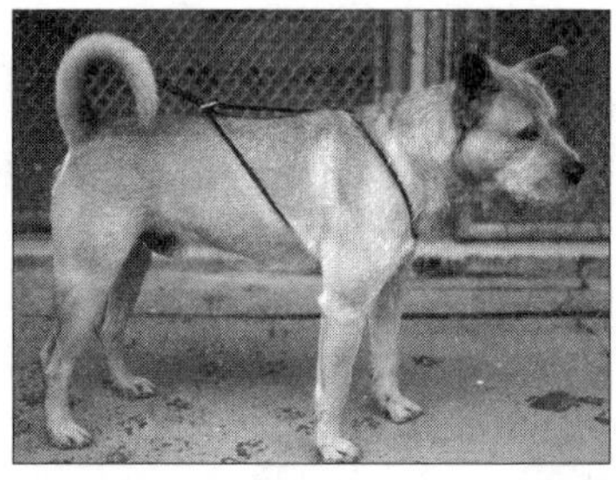

The Holt Harness is made of soft, braided nylon, with sturdy hardware. An elasticized band cushions the chest to minimize rubbing. Though confusing to put on the dog the first time, once you figure it out it is simple to use.

Our consulting trainer tested this device on several dogs and found that tolerance and effectiveness was high. Unlike the headcollar, most dogs did not need an "acclimatization period." Four out of six shelter dogs tested (of various sizes and temperaments) responded well and immediately reduced their pulling. But a stressed and hyperactive Rottweiler barely seemed to notice the harness, and the last dog, a wiry terrier mix, almost managed to escape the harness. He was effectively stopped from pulling, but minutes later, changed his tactics to include spinning and trying to grab the leash snapped to the harness. This tack was successful for him; the harness affords precious little ability to control the dog unless he pulls straight away from the handler, and his playful, exuberant spinning and jumping quickly got him tangled up. If your dog is a straight-away, enthusiastic puller, this product would probably work really well.

Pro-Stop! Harness

This harness works on a principle similar to that of the Holt, but with a twist. Here, the corrective tightening comes from padded leg straps wrapped around the dog's front legs instead of around the chest. The location of the straps (above the dog's front elbows,

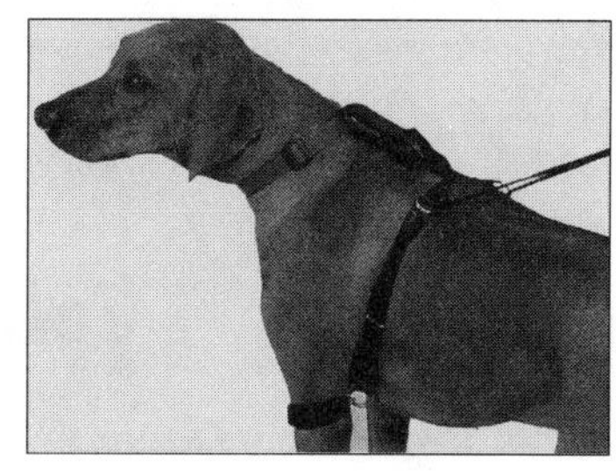

high in his armpits) appears very uncomfortable for any dog, even if it's not pulling against its restraint.

This product was more effective on our Rottweiler, but a sweet Australian Shepherd and a submissive black Labrador were befuddled by the pressure on their legs. Sensitive dogs might get too distracted to enjoy a walk while wearing this harness and may even injure themselves.

The Right Choice

Any collar, but particularly a choke collar, is potentially dangerous if left on an unsupervised dog. The very design of the choke collar makes it easier for a dog to strangle himself, since the dangling ring can catch on objects causing the dog to panic and hang himself.

The design of both the buckle and pinch collars make it more difficult to catch the rings on objects. Neither pinch collar nor buckle collar is designed to tighten as the choke does. Still, be aware that if a dog catches the collar, the dog can strangle, no matter what kind of collar it is wearing. So which is the best collar? It's the one with which you get the type of cooperation you want from your dog.

You should be able to control and work with your dog without constantly "reminding" him what to do. Nagging a dog on a choke collar, or any collar, should indicate to you that your dog is ignoring your corrections. In essence you are effectively training the dog to ignore you—just as a human being would in the same "nagging" situation. Continuous jerking, whether in a buckle or slip collar hints that another type of collar, training method, or tool should be implemented.

We favor the head harness because it fits in with a positive-reinforcement style of training. Says Dr. Dodman: "If we can train a killer whale to launch itself out of a swimming pool, roll on it's side and urinate in a small plastic cup with a whistle and a bucket of fish as a reward, we should be able to train a domestic dog to do anything you want to with equivalent positive reinforcement." Have you ever seen a trainer at Sea World *spank* a dolphin?

The bottom line should be to use the *mildest* collar that gives the results you need. If that's a simple, inexpensive buckle collar or a halter, you are far, far ahead of the game. Dodman says, "If you use the right reward for the right dog, and it isn't always food, you will have a dog who will respond over 85 percent of the time, which is all the average domestic dog ever needs. If people use collars suitable for positive training, such as halters, they're going to have happier dogs, and they'll be happier owners as well."

Collar Savvy

■ ***Preventing Dependence**: No matter what type of training collar you use, try to make sure your dog doesn't become dependent on it. Dogs associate a learned behavior (such as walking calmly by your side) with the device used during the learning process. Thus, if you replace a training collar with an everyday collar, your dog may pull once again.*

You can avoid "device dependence" by always rewarding your dog for appropriate behavior and by gradually weaning your dog off its training collar.

■ ***Appropriate Fit**: Proper fit is important with any collar. When dogs wear buckle collars too loosely, they can back out of them. To prevent this, keep the collar tight enough so you can fit only two fingers under the collar comfortably. Choke collars are most effective when worn high on the neck, right behind the ears. Always follow manufacturer's instructions when fitting head halters and body harnesses.*

■ ***On or Off?** While it's advisable for your dog to wear a collar most of the time, there are times when Bowser should shed his neckwear.*

Because choke and buckle collars can snag and strangle a dog, consider removing such collars when your dog's at home or in the yard unsupervised. And remove any collar or halter when your dog is in its crate.

Lowdown on Leashes

Leashes present fewer choices than collars, and there are fewer professional differences of opinion about them. Generally, a 6-foot leash is best for training or routine walks. Longer leads are useful for outdoor training—especially when teaching the "come" command. But be aware that in some communities a dog is considered "at large" if it's at the end of a leash longer than 6 feet.

Canvas or leather leashes are easiest on your hands. Make sure the clip is strong but not so big that it slaps your dog while walking. Retractable leashes are increasingly popular, but their long length and extendability encourage pulling. Plus, getting tangled in the thin cord can injure a dog or its handler.

Remember, dog tack is a management tool, not a crutch. Nothing works better than praise and kindness to encourage your dog to stay by your side. The ultimate goal is to have your dog focused on you—not on what's around its neck.

Besides, dogs who strain at their leashes (and who subsequently get jerked by their frustrated handlers) are more likely to have spinal misalignments, and dogs with spinal problems have a much higher incidence of aggressive and/or hyperactive behavior problems.two

Below are two leash evaluations based on the following five criteria: Effectiveness; dogs' acceptance of the product; humaneness of the concept; quality of manufacture, and cost.

One important caveat: All no-pull products are most effective when used as a temporary behavior management tool while the dog is taught to walk on a leash. Several work on an aversive (positive punishment) principal, whereby the dog's behavior (pulling) makes something "bad" happen, in this case, discomfort.*Unless the owner rewards and reinforces the desirable behavior, (walking politely) the dog may become acclimatized to increasing levels of discomfort, and the product loses its effectiveness.*

Sof-Touch Training Safety Leash

Developed by well-known behaviorist William Campbell, the Sof-Touch is a simple six-foot nylon leash with a short piece of elastic stitched and snapped in, to create a shock-absorber in the leash. the leash comes in a one-half-inch width for small dogs, and three-quarter-inch width for larger dogs.

The leash administers its own correction, but because the leash itself is solid nylon, there is not nearly as much bounce-back effect as the next elasticized leash we'll discuss. In the Sof-Touch, the elastic piece tightens gradually, muting the impact of the dog hitting the end of the leash. Even if an owner resorts to a jerk on the leash,

the elastic adds the same muted effect to the correction.

This leash works best in conjunction with a positive reinforcement program that trains the dog not to pull by rewarding polite walking with an encouraging,"Yes!"and a treat.

The Elasta-Leash

The Elasta-Leash is an extremely sturdy, well-made leash much like a thick, four-foot bungee cord attached to your dog's collar. When the dog hits the end of the leash, it literally "twangs" him back. There is no question that it checks the dog's pulling—the harder the dog hits the end of the leash, the harder he bounces back.

Our test dogs included an Australian Shepherd who only needed three mild twangs to stop pulling, an adolescent Doberman mix who did well only after a reward was added to the process (Yes! and a treat) and a Jack Russell Terrier, who could have kept bouncing off the end of the leash *ad nauseum*.

Since the leash administers the twang rather than the handler, the timing of the correction is always perfect. The elastic quality of the leash reduces the force of the correction on the dog's throat, so it is less likely to do damage to the trachea.

However, the leash still administers a pretty strong correction that cannot in any way be considered a positive reinforcement solution to the leash-pulling problem and we do not recommend it.

Another Solution

Dennis Fetko, Ph.D., a San Diego-based dog trainer and applied animal behaviorist, advocates a simple way to cure dogs of pulling on lead. The method works with any type of collar (though he prefers a close-fitting nylon slip collar) and doesn't involve any jerking or tugging.

"Whenever you feel tension on the lead from your dog pulling, stop dead in your tracks," advises Dr. Fetko. Don't move until your dog turns around or backs up to put slack back in the leash. Only then should you praise your dog and continue walking. "Your dog will learn quickly that a slack leash, not pulling, will get it what it wants—forward progress," says Dr. Fetko.

19

Headcollars

The headcollar works on dogs just like a halter works on horses. It's also a smart, gentle way to alter your dog's troubling behavior.

Meet Beau, the Bouvier des Flandres. When he arrived for the first night of obedience class with his owner, Beau was anxious to get out of the car and romp with the other dogs in class – typical behavior for a normal, socialized 18-month-old pup. However, Beau the 80-pound Bouvier became Beau the kangaroo, leaping wildly around the parking lot with his 120-pound female human in tow. The heavy-duty choke collar Beau was wearing had little effect in stopping this behavior.

The reason? Beau seldom got to go on walks. The owner's husband was the only family member who had the strength to "handle" Beau, and he was not especially motivated to assume this daily task. Consequently, most of Beau's time was spent in the garage or at the end of a 20-foot rope attached to the corner of the house.

Beau's behavior is very common. In group classes with dogs and puppies, more than half arrive pulling and lunging so hard they choke themselves and yank their owners around. And it isn't just the big breeds: West Highland Terriers gag and strangle themselves, and Miniature Dachshunds pull so hard their paws are raw.

This condition tends to worsen over time, as taking the dog for a walk becomes less and less enjoyable for the human at the end of the leash, resulting in less frequent and shorter walks. The problem is compounded when the dog walker has a back, shoulder, or elbow problem, or arthritis. Walking an out-of-control dog is not only unpleasant for these people, but it is dangerous as well.

A Practical Solution

The solution is called a "headcollar," and it works on dogs like a halter works on horses. Headcollars have a strap that fits over the nose of the dog, so that you lead them from the head, not the neck. Just as with bigger, stronger animals like horses or bulls, by controlling the head, you control the whole dog.

At first glance, the loop that fits over the dog's nose may give the appearance of a muzzle. Actually, the loop allows the dog freedom to open his mouth to eat, drink, pant, even carry a toy. As long as the dog maintains a loose leash, he is free to open his mouth. But if he tries to pull, or lunge, or bite, the headcollar turns his head and prevents the problem – and the person on the other end of the leash doesn't have to pull hard to achieve this effect! In most cases, even young children or elderly people can lead large dogs who were previously unmanageable. It takes much less effort to control the nose of the dog than to control the powerful neck muscles.

A training priority is to use methods that are fun and non-aggressive, so the dog receives positive input. The tendency for many people when using choke chains or pinch collars is to constantly tug and yank on their dogs. Over time the dogs learn to ignore the signal. Even when used as designed, choke chains and pinch collars inflict pain to control behavior. Yanking on pinch collars and choke chains when a dog is aggressive around other people or dogs only adds to the negative experience. And suppressing this behavior through painful means does not change the dog's attitude.

With a headcollar, however, the correction for pulling isn't pain, but displacement. Every time the dog tries to pull away, his head is turned back toward the handler. He cannot lean into or overwhelm the strength of the person holding his leash. Under these circumstances, most dogs immediately cease pulling.

Headcollars should never be used, however, for tying up a dog or for constant wear. They are strictly for training, and should be removed promptly when the dog's training or exercise session is completed.

But if owners realize they can walk their dogs without a struggle, they will walk them more often, resulting in better behavior both on the walks and at home. Going for regular walks helps dogs burn off excess energy and is a great way for dogs and people to form stronger bonds. Walking also gives you an opportunity to introduce your dog to lots of new sights and sounds and teach him appropriate behavior.

As for Beau, by the end of the six-week training session his owner couldn't believe he was the same dog. Even the kids in his family were happy to take Beau with them on walks—not only on the back roads but also into town. He became a welcome member of his family again.

JUST AS WITH BIGGER, STRONGER ANIMALS LIKE HORSES OR BULLS, BY CONTROLLING THE HEAD, YOU CONTROL THE WHOLE DOG.

Battle-tested

The first night of any beginning level dog training class can be chaotic. For many people, this is their first time in a group class and often with their first dog. Owners get dragged through the parking lot. Dogs bark and lunge at other dogs. Owners' faces reflect utter relief and amazement after their dogs are fitted with head collars. Within five minutes the dogs are calm, quiet, and under control.

The headcollar also allows you to teach a dog to behave in distracting situations. Exposing a dog to different stimulating situations helps him to calm down and walk without pulling. Many dogs are able to return to wearing a regular buckle collar after just a few months of learning how to control themselves with the headcollar.

How To Fit Your Dog's Headcollar

Using a headcollar to control a dog's head and mouth enables you to keep even the most excitable dog under control, without causing the dog any pain. However, if your dog is aggressive toward people or other dogs, Contact a qualified trainer/behaviorist to assist you.

When properly introduced, it only takes few minutes, or at most, a couple of short sessions for the dog to accept a headcollar. Proper fit is very important for comfort and for your dog's acceptance of the head collar. It should fit comfortably without restricting use of the mouth when the leash is loose.

When putting a headcollar on a dog for the first time, give him a yummy treat as he pokes his head through the loop. He will quickly see he has full use of his mouth for eating, and it will give him some incentive for doing it again.

Right after putting on the headcollar, distract the dog while he adjusts to how it feels. Then take the dog for a short walk. If he continues to struggle, encourage him to walk beside you by patting your leg and verbally encouraging him to come along. It is helpful to use treats to get him to stay near your side as you walk.

This allows the dog to learn that if he maintains slack in the leash, the headcollar remains open and he is free to explore the length of his leash, whether it is a retractable leash or a six-foot leash.

Choosing the Right Headcollar

Following are evaluations of three styles of headcollars. Although the designs differ, the concept of leading from the head is the same. While each has its advantages due to subtle design differences, ultimately the success of each depends on how well it fits the shape of the dog's head and nose.

Gentle Leader

The Gentle Leader was developed by Dr. R. K. Anderson (Professor and Director Emeritus of the Animal Behavior Clinic at the University of Minnesota) and Dr. Ruth Foster (past president of the National Association of Dog Obedience Instructors). They feel that having a trained person fit and teach the dog and its owner is the best way to guarantee success, so Gentle Leaders are sold only through dog trainers and veterinarians.

Of the three models, the Gentle Leader is the only one without side straps, as well as the only one with a non-tightening nose loop. That means once you adjust the headcollar, it moves around on the dog's head less than the other two models – good for sensitive dogs, since its simpler design gives them less collar to be aware of. Note, however, that the tightening action of the nose loop is distracting to some dogs, and unneccesary to teach most dogs to stop pulling.

Snoot Loop

The Snoot Loop was developed by Peter L. Borchelt, Ph.D., an Applied Animal Behaviorist certified by the Animal Behavior Society. Borchelt is also the director of the Animal Behavior Clinic at the Animal Medical Center in New York.

The Snoot Loop's design makes it the easiest headcollar to adjust for fit. Its side straps, connecting the neck loop and the nose loop, are adjustable, making it easier to fit dogs that have a big head and a short "snoot."

The petite size is the answer for hard-to-fit toy breeds such as Yorkshire Terriers and Miniature Pinschers. Dr. Borchelt has another Snoot Loop designed especially for breeds such as the Pug and Bulldog. And, if you purchase a Snoot Loop that cannot be adjusted to fit correctly, the company will custom-make one to fit.

The Snoot Loop's straps are made out of the narrowest material of the three headcollars. This means that when a dog pulls against it, the pressure it exerts on the dog's nose is sharper than the pressure exerted by the wider straps of the other two brands. The loose weave of the material makes the threads apt to snag if the dog paws at the headcollar.

Halti

The Halti headcollar was designed by Dr. Roger Mugford in England. Like the Snoot Loop, the Halti has side straps that improve the fit of the headcollar, but the Halti's side straps are not adjustable. Both the nylon material and the hardware (metal rings) of the Halti are sturdier than that of the Snoot Loop, however.

An added bonus is that the Halti seems to be the most widely distributed headcollar on the market; most large pet stores carry this brand.

For additional details on headcollars, see Appendix.

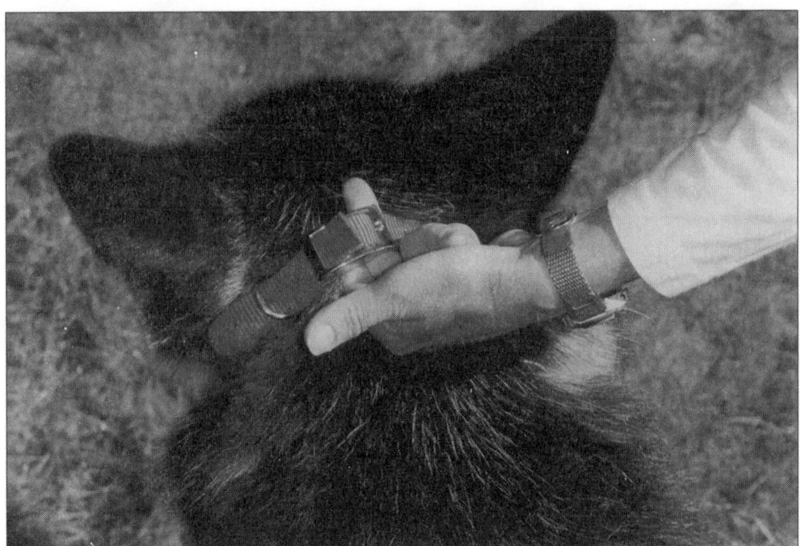

Above, Before putting the nose loop around the dog's nose, get the neck strap fitted correctly. Without using the nose loop, fasten and adjust this strap so that it is high and snug, close behind the dog's ears. It should be tight enough that only one finger can fit between the strap and the dog. Below, Next, take the neck strap off, and teach your dog to put his nose through the nose loop. Feed him a treat as he pokes his nose through. Then fasten the neck strap, which is already adjusted to the correct tightness. Distract the dog with a little play after you fasten the headcollar.

Headcollars work by turning the dog's head in your direction when you gently pull on the leash. With a properly adjusted headcollar, you will never have to yank or pull hard. Above, The nose loop of the Gentle Leader, has an adjustment under the dog's jaw. The nose loop should slide from just underneath the dog's eyes almost to the tip of his nose. With adult dogs, you only have to adjust the straps the first time you use the headcollar. But with growing puppies, check the fit every time it's used. Below, The nose loop should cross just behind the corner of the dog's mouth so he has full use of his mouth.

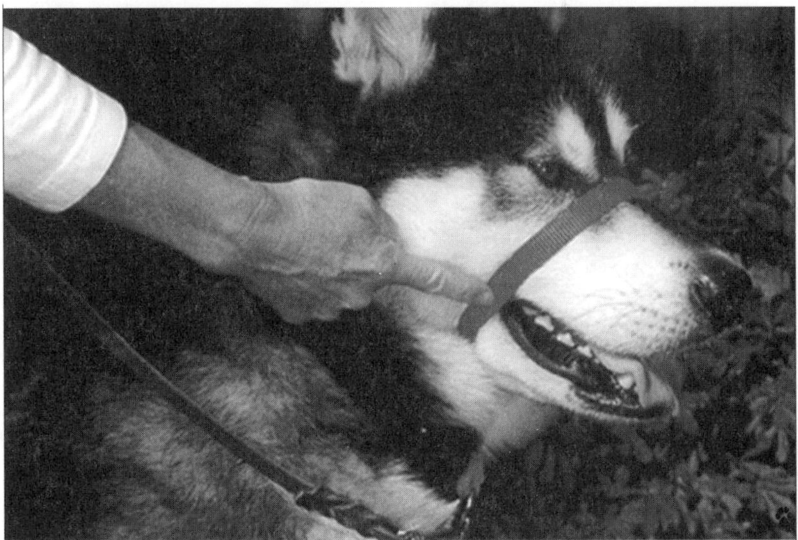

20

Electronic Fences

An old-fashioned, solid fence, good training and sufficient exercise are still the best bets. But here's the lowdown.

With more than ten years' field experience under his belt, the veteran humane officer, from Santa Clara County, California, thought he had seen and heard just about everything. Then he got the call from a hysterical woman who had come home from work to find that her dog was being shocked non-stop by his electronic collar.

"Please hurry," she begged. "He's totally crazed, and when we try to touch him we get shocked. We can't get the collar off him!"

The officer rushed to the scene. When he arrived he found that the owners had managed to throw a rug over the dog, restrain him, and cut off the offending collar with a knife. The dog was still so severely traumatized by the experience that he refused to allow anyone near. The woman vowed never to use her underground fence system again.

Electronic fences and their partners—collars that deliver an aversive agent – have been around for more than 20 years. They seem like the perfect canine confinement alternative to a solid physical fence. They are often marketed as the ideal fencing solution to homeowner association fence prohibitions and for problematic, difficult-to-fence, steep, rocky, and rugged living spaces.

But while occurrences such as the one described above are relatively rare, there are other drawbacks to using electronic fencing systems. A conscientious owner will weigh all the pros and cons before deciding whether or not to invest in this sort of "fencing" system.

How Do They Work?

Electronic fences rely on the transmission of a radio signal from a wire or some other transmitter that is typically buried or mounted in an unobtrusive location on the dog owner's property. The radio signal is broadcast within a specific zone, following the contours of the individual layout. The dog wears a battery-operated receiver on a special collar, which picks up the radio signals when the dog enters the special zone. Most of the systems are programmed so that a "warning tone" is emitted when the dog first approaches the radio transmission area, and, if he remains or travels further into the zone, follows up with an aversive stimulus.

The most commonly used aversive is an electric shock, delivered to the dog's neck by metal (electrically conducting) prongs set in the dog's collar. A recent technological innovation provides for some systems to deliver a burst of citronella spray as the aversive instead of an electric shock.

The best of the electronic fence makers teach the dog owners how to condition their dogs to the fence. "Training flags" are installed around the perimeter of the dog's "safe" territory, to give him a visual hint to its shape and size. For the first few days, it is suggested that the owner applies tape over the prongs on the electrical collar, to minimize any shock that the dog receives, and to keep the dog on a leash. The owner is instructed to walk around the property, allowing the dog to approach the forbidden zones and hear the warning tone. The owner is to pull or call the dog back into the safe area, and then praise the dog.

The next phase involves removing the tape, and allowing the dog (who is still on a leash) farther into the danger zone, where he experiences a correction. Again, the owner brings the dog back into the safety zone, praising his retreat from the forbidden area. This is followed by a few more days of off-leash, but supervised, experiences, and finally, removal of the training flags. Whether the aversive is a shock or spray, in most cases it takes only a few applications for the dog to learn that the tone means "Bad things happen here."

Advantages Of "Virtual" Fences

There are certainly advantages to electronic fences. They are generally less expensive than a physical fence. Systems range in cost from $120 to $400, and can cover terrain ranging from a small yard to a 100-acre parcel, depending on the brand. Variation in cost depends in large part on the features included in the system package, such as adjustable levels of shock strength, rechargeable batteries, and combination fence and no-bark or fence and remote trainer systems. If you are considering investing in an electronic fence, compare features carefully in order to get the brand that best suits your needs.

Electronic fences also are easier to install than a traditional fence. One system uses a wire that is buried a few inches underground, a process that is much less labor-intensive than digging post holes and building fences, especially in rocky soil or on steep brushy slopes. Another type of fence doesn't even require a buried wire, but instead uses transmitters on "emitter posts" that are inserted into the ground at intervals around the property. Consumers can install the fences themselves, or hire one of the many landscapers and builders who have experience in underground fence installation. Some companies will provide a list of certified fence installers on request.

For those who simply prefer the aesthetics of a fenceless yard or are faced with homeowner association constraints, electronic fences can keep a dog contained without obstructing the view or violating neighborhood sensibilities.

The Negative Side

Paul Miller, now director of the Chattanooga Animal Services program in Tennessee, was the Santa Clara humane officer who responded to the call of a dog being shocked by his collar a decade ago. Ten more years of experience in the field haven't softened his opinion of the product. He argues that electronic fences don't provide adequate containment to reasonably guarantee a dog's safety.

"I can't tell you exactly how many stray dogs I've seen wearing electronic fence collars," he says, "but it's a lot. Owners forget to replace weak and dying batteries and dogs are soon free to come and go at will. Many owners who come in to shelters to retrieve their shock-collared wayward hounds will admit that they were aware the batteries were weak and they hadn't bothered to replace them."

Another minus: Some dogs seem to have no trouble braving the strong corrections imposed on them by a working collar with fresh batteries if they are presented with sufficiently enticing stimuli: a female in season, a fast-moving cat, a child on a bicycle, a postal worker. And then the dog is stuck outside the fence without sufficient motivation to risk the shock to get back in! For this reason, certain breeds, especially large dogs bred for guardian jobs or dogs with strong hunting drives, make poor candidates for these systems.

Another important consideration is the fact that an electronic fence does nothing to protect your dog from outside harm. The neighborhood canine bully can still enter your yard and attack your dog. Bad people can still come onto your property and steal or torment your dog. (We've even heard one report of an expensive electronic collar being stolen right off its dog!) Also, these electronic fences don't keep children or delivery people from approaching your house and being attacked or bitten by your dog.

Finally, dogs with especially long or thick coats may have to have their necks shaved in order for the prongs (and the corrective shocks) to reach their skin. Such disfigurement is not acceptable to all owners.

"Mild" Is A Matter of Opinion

Dog owners also need to be concerned about the unintended negative side effects of punishment. Despite the euphemisms used in promotional materials that call the aversive electric shock a "mild electrical stimulus," a "stimulus distraction," a "tingle," or a "tickle," it is, in fact, an electric shock.

In November 1998, at the Association of Pet Dog Trainers annual conference and trade show in Valley Forge, Pennsylvania, a number of dog trainers tested an electric collar by wrapping it around their own hands. (The equipment was provided by one of the electronic fence manufacturers, who had a trade booth at the convention.) Different people reacted to varying levels of shock with significantly different levels of sensitivity. While some felt nothing at the lowest setting and only a mild sensation at level three, others described a mildly painful sensation at level one and unpleasant, even intolerable pain at the higher settings. (The shock was felt on the hand, not on the more sensitive neck area. Product representatives refused to allow the human Guinea pigs to test the collars on their necks.) There is every reason to think that our dogs would also have different sensitivities to electric shocks.

The use of punishment in training, especially a punishment as intense as an electric shock, risks irreparable harm to the mutual trust that is critically important in the dog-human relationship. During the training process, the dog may associate the shock or spray with the owner's presence and end up fearing the owner.

Sensitive dogs can be seriously traumatized by just one administration of the punishing aversive. Some dogs may refuse to enter the yard at all after being shocked or sprayed, especially if the yard is small, with a limited amount of "free" space where the dog can feel safe. One Monterey County, California dog owner reports that while she loves the electronic fence system because it allows her dogs to run loose on her several-acre property (which she couldn't otherwise afford to fence), her Komondor is so respectful of the boundary that the dog won't cross it even when not wearing the collar. The owner has to load her dog into the car and drive across the wire just to take the dog for a walk around the neighborhood.

THERE IS NOTHING THAT CAN REPLACE TRAINING, SUPERVISION, AND ... A PURELY "VISIBLE," SOLID, WELL-MAINTAINED FENCE.

What Are The Alternatives?

What are you supposed to do if you live in an area where fencing is prohibited, prohibitively expensive, or simply not feasible? You can keep Rover in the house, train him to come when called, and allow him outside only under direct supervision. You can install a cable runner, although tying a dog up creates its own set of risks and problems. You can purchase a chain-link kennel run to provide safe confinement for Rover when you aren't able to personally supervise his exercise. Or you can move to a neighborhood that allows physical fences.

Some people, however, feel the benefits of an electronic fence system outweigh the negatives of the alternatives. We'd grudgingly acknowledge the potential usefulness of the system, provided it's used in the following limited circumstances.

Because of the potential for an electronic fence to malfunction, for your dog to simply "run through" it and escape, and for predators to enter your property and injure your dog, we suggest using the system only when you are home and able to monitor its use. This means not using the system when you are not at home (even just for a few minutes), or at night (or any other time you may be sleeping). You must check on your dog constantly, establishing visual contact with him at least every five minutes or so when he is "confined" by the fence and nothing else. And the collar must be removed whenever the fence is not being used as the primary barrier (when the dog is safely confined in the house, for instance). Failing to do all these things exposes the dog to the dangers discussed above, while simultaneously giving the owner a false sense of security.

Of course, if your dog is reliably trained to come to you when he is called and you are keeping him under this sort of close supervision, you probably don't need this sort of system! Which strikes at the heart of our objections to electronic fences: They are really designed as a "convenience" device for people who like having a dog, and who don't want it to run away, but who are unwilling or unable to go the extra mile to absolutely ensure the safety of their dogs.

There are exceptions. There are dog owners, for instance, who keep their well-trained dogs under close supervision, but who maintain the electronic fence as a sort of "emergency back up" barrier for their dogs because they live on a busy road, and even an extremely rare, quick trip "off the property" could result in death.

In our opinion, however, there is nothing that can replace training, supervision, and that timeless tool for good neighbors everywhere: a purely "visible," solid, well-maintained fence.

Fence Features Comparison

■ ***Invisible Fence****: The Invisible Fence (IF) was the first underground electronic fence to appear on the market some 25 years ago. It is marketed only through IF dealers, and each system is totally customized.*

■ ***Innotek Pet Containment Systems****: Innotek offers a wide variety of features, from their K9 Economy system, which covers up to three acres and has a variable warning zone from one foot to 25 feet.*

HF-201 deluxe system: three levels of shock, variable warning zone (one - 25 ft.), low-battery indicator on collar, lightning protection, run-through protection (automatically increases shock level if the dog travels more than one-third the distance into the warning zone), and over-correction protection (turns off the shock after a period of time if the dog gets trapped in the correction zone.

Innotek also sells two combined systems: Bark 'N' Contain that combines an electronic fence and no-bark collar in one unit and Contain 'N' Train which combines an electronic fence and hand-held remote trainer in one unit.

■ ***Radio Fence***: *Like Innotek, Radio Fence offers a spectrum of features at a range of prices from the Standard System (for a small to average-sized yard) to the Deluxe System (covers up to 100 acres) to their Instant Fence Wireless system–a portable above-ground system with a transmission radius of 100 feet.*

Their underground fence collars are available in "Ultralight" for the sensitive dog, "Standard" for the average dog, and "Stubborn Dog." (Editor's note: Dogs are not inherently "stubborn." Dogs who have been labeled as "stubborn" usually belong to people who have not learned how to adequately communicate with and/or motive the dog, or are looking for a "quick fix.")

Radio Fence collars are adjustable for "tone only," "tone and shock," or "shock only," but the intensity level of the shock is not adjustable.

Radio Fence also offers an underground Citronella Fence system Citronella is a strong-smelling non-toxic oil from a fragrant Asiatic grass that smells like lemon.

■ ***Animal Behavior Systems, In****c.*: *Animal Behaviors Systems, Inc., is the originator of citronella training systems in the United States. Because of their commitment to humane training products and methods, they market their underground Virtual Fence and other citronella training products only through animal care professionals such as veterinarians, trainers, and shelters. This way, they believe, pet owners will purchase and use the product with the guidance of a professional who can make sure they are using it correctly.*

For information on locating these products, see Appendix. ❖

Appendix

Agility
American Kennel Club (AKC)
5580 Centerview Dr. Suite 200
Raleigh, NC 27606
(919) 233-9780

United Kennel Club
100 E. Kilgore Rd.
Kalamazoo, MI 49001
(616) 343-9020

North American Dog Agility Council
HCR 2 Box 277
St. Maries, ID 83861

U. S. Dog Agility Association
P.O. Box 850955
Richardson, TX 75085-0955
(972) 231-9700

Herding
Australian Shepherd Club of America
6091 Hwy 21
Bryan, TX 77803-9652
(409) 778-1082

American Herding Breed Association
AHBA Secretary
1548 Victoria Way
Pacifica, CA 94044

U.S. Border Collie Handler's Association
Francis Raley, Secretary
2915 Anderson Ln.
Crawford, TX 76638
(254) 486-2500

AKC Test/Trial Program
51 Madison Ave.
New York, NY 10010

Flyball
NAFA, Inc.
1002 E. Sanuel Ave.
Peoria Heights, IL 61614

Frisbee
Alpo Canine Frisbee Disc Champ.
Peter Bloeme, Director
4060 - D Peachtree Rd.
Suite 326M
Atlanta, GA 03019

Therapy Certification
Delta Society, Pet Partners
P.O. Box 1080
Renton, WA 98057
(800) 869-6898

Therapy Dogs International
6 Hilltop Rd.
Mendham, NJ 07945a
(201) 543-0888

Freestyle
Sharon Tutt
Treasurer/Membership
1665 Parkview Place
Surrey, B. C.
Canada, V4N 1Y8
(604) 581-3641

Joan Stevenson
22 Roanoke Rd.
Matawan, NJ 07747
(908) 566-3812

Tracking
American Kennel Club
5580 Centerview Dr.
Suite 200
Raleigh, NC 27606
(919) 233-9780

United Schutzhund Clubs of America
3810 Paule Ave.
St. Louis, MO 63125-1718

Australian Shepherd Club of America
6091 E. State Hwy. 21
Bryan, TX 78808
(409) 778-1082

American Mixed Breed Obedience
Registry (AMBOR)
P.O. Box 7841
Rockford, IL 61126-7841

Canadian Kennel Club
100-89 Skyway Ave., Unit 100
Etobicoke, Ontario M

Electric Fences

■ Invisible Fence: (IF) was the first underground electronic fence to appear on the market some 25 years ago. It is marketed only through IF dealers, and each system is totally customized. A list of dealers is available on the IF website (www.ifco.com). In the US, call (800) 538-3647; in Canada, call (800) 661-6286.

■ Innotek Pet Containment Systems: Innotek offers a wide variety of features, from their K9 Economy system, which covers up to three acres and has a variable warning zone from one foot to 25 feet (on sale at their web site for $119.95), to their Home Free-201 System, which covers up to 25 acres for pets up to 200 pounds ($248).

The HF-201 deluxe system has three levels of shock, variable warning zone from one foot to 25 feet, a low-battery indicator on the collar, lightning protection, run-through protection that automatically increases the shock level if your dog has traveled more than one-third the distance into the warning zone, and over-correction protection that turns off the shock after a period of time if your dog gets trapped in the "correction zone."

Innotek also sells two combined systems: Bark 'N' Contain that combines an electronic fence and no-bark collar in one unit ($290), and Contain 'N' Train which combines an electronic fence and hand-held remote trainer in one unit ($290). More information: www.pet-products.com or call Innotek Pet Products: (800) 826-5527.

■ Radio Fence: Like Innotek, Radio Fence offers a spectrum of features at a range of prices from $105 for their Standard System (for a small to average-sized yard) and $187 for the Deluxe System (covers up to 100 acres) to their Instant Fence Wireless system, at $355 – a portable above-ground system with a transmission radius of 100 feet. Their underground fence collars are available in "Ultralight" for the sensitive dog, "Standard" for the average dog, and "Stubborn Dog." (Editor's note: Dogs are not inherently "stubborn." Dogs who have been labeled as "stubborn" usually belong to people who have not learned how to adequately communicate with and/or motive the dog, or are looking for a "quick fix.") Radio Fence collars are adjustable for "tone only," "tone and shock," or "shock only," but the intensity level of the shock is not adjustable.

Radio Fence also offers an underground Citronella Fence system ($177). Citronella is a strong-smelling non-toxic oil from a fragrant Asiatic grass that smells like lemon. More information: www.radiofence.com or call Radio Fence at (800) 941-4200 or (941) 505-8220.

Animal Behavior Systems

ABS is the originator of citronella training systems in the United States. The products only through animal care professionals such as veterinarians, trainers, and shelters.

ABS offers trainers and dog owners an alternative that uses non-shocking devices to humanely manage and correct a variety of unacceptable dog behaviors. Each of the ABS behavior management products utilizes the same basic technology —the dog wears a nylon collar with a sensor unit attached, and a pressurized reservoir filled with citronella. When the sensor unit is triggered it releases a brisk citronella spray-burst in front of the dog's nose.

The spray is a natural, non-toxic liquid that distracts the dog from the inappropriate behavior and acts as a mild aversive. (The odor is pleasing to most humans and is also commonly used to repel mosquitoes, so it coincidentally acts as a natural air freshener and mosquito repellent!) The dog hears, sees, feels and smells the spray and finds the experience distasteful, and soon learns which behaviors to stop in order to avoid triggering the spray.

■ ABS Anti-Barking System is the original citronella collar product. With this collar, the sensing unit is triggered by the sound of the dog barking. The dog soon realizes that the spray is triggered whenever he barks, and in a short while chooses to remain quiet. The Anti-Bark Kit consists of the adjustable collar, one can of citronella, a 6-

volt alkaline battery and detailed instructions. It is available in two sizes — the larger, approximately five ounces, is recommended for dogs 15 pounds or over. The smaller two ounce size is best for toy-sized dogs. The collar unit is simple to assemble and use, and has two settings so that trigger sensitivity can be adjusted according to need. Clinical studies reportedly found the collar's effectiveness to be near 90 percent. Our consulting trainer reports a similar success rate, and givesit a definite "paws up."

■ ABS Indoor Area Avoidance System (IAAS) is used to keep dogs away from an "off-limits" designated piece of furniture, room, or other area inside the house, utilizing the same citronella technology. It is activated by a radio wave from a transmitter which is matched to the receiver collar worn by the dog. The transmitter can be adjusted to create a circular radio-wave barrier from a two- to 20-foot radius. When a dog approaches within two feet of the barrier she first hears an audible tone warning. If she continues forward, she receives a spray of citronella every five seconds until she retreats. If she remains inside the barrier the audible tone changes and increases in frequency, and the device continues to spray every three to five seconds.

In order for an area-avoidance device to be most effective, it needs to be triggered by the dog's behavior even in the owner's absence, reset itself so it can work repeatedly, and present an aversive that elicits the desired response in the dog without causing panic or undue stress. The IAAS meets these criteria and also receives a "paws up."

■ ABS Outdoor Area Avoidance System (OAAS) utilizes the same citronella spray and radio wave barrier as the indoor system. The difference is that the outdoor system has a wire that can be buried in the ground, and cover several acres.

This type of system (using electric shock) has been marketed for several years as a "virtual fence" dog containment system. However, ABS believes the system is better used as area avoidance (to keep your dog out of the garden, or away from livestock or poultry), rather than confinement. We think the virtual fence systems present serious safety concerns when used as a primary means of confinement for a dog, and recommends the OAAS as an avoidance system only, not for primary confinement.

■ ABS Remote Trainer incorporates the same technology as the anti-bark system, with one exception. The difference is that the spray is activated by a remote radio signal from a hand-held device triggered by the person training the dog. It is useful for getting a dog's attention during training, and can deliver either a short or long spray. When using an aversive correction in training it is important that it be done properly.

Timing is critical, and any correction needs to be followed by eliciting appropriate behavior that can be rewarded. An aversive used improperly loses its effectiveness as the dog becomes acclimated to it, especially if acceptable behavior is not established in place of the inappropriate behavior that is interrupted by the aversive. For this reason, ABS suggests and we concur that the Remote Trainer be used only under the guidance of a skilled professional trainer or animal behaviorist

ABS Behavior Management Systems are available through veterinarians, trainers and animal shelters. For a distributor near you, contact Animal Behavior Systems, Inc. at 1-800-627-9447 or have your animal care professional contact ABS.

Collars & Leads

■ The Holt Control Harness comes in small, medium and large, fits neck sizes 8-26 inches, and is available from most pet supply catalogs and stores for about $10. This product is worth trying, especially for dogs who don't like headcollars.

■ The Pro-Stop! Harness is well-made, but more complicated to put on the dog than the Holt Harness. It's also more expensive – $15-20. It doesn't adjust for tiny dogs, but accommodates larger sizes (up to 42" girth) than the Holt Harness.

■ The Pro-Stop! Harness is well-made, but more complicated to put on the dog than the Holt Harness. It's also more expensive – $15-20. It doesn't adjust for tiny dogs, but accommodates larger sizes (up to 42" girth) than the Holt Harness.

n The Sof-Touch leash is an affordable $12 (less for quantity orders) from William E. Campbell, at (541) 476-5775.

■ The Gentle Leader comes in a variety of colors, and sizes range from Petite (dogs and puppies with an adult weight under five pounds) to Extra-Large (130 pounds or more). It retails for $16 to $25. Premier Pet Products, 527 Branchway Road, Richmond, VA 23236; phone (804) 379-4702; fax (804) 379-0403; www.gentleleader.com.

■ The Snoot Loop comes in five sizes ranging from Petite to Large, but only in black. It retails for $16 to $20. Contact Dr. Borchelt 2465 Stuart Street, Brooklyn, NY 11229; phone (800) 339-9505 or (718) 891-4200; fax (718) 769-9394.

■ The Halti is available only in black and retails for $16-$20. Sizes range from Size 0 (Miniature Dachshund, Papillon, Toy Poodle, Yorkshire Terrier) to Size 5 (St. Bernard, Mastiffs, Great Danes). Contact Coastal at 911 Leadway Avenue, Alliance, OH 44601; phone (800) 321-0248 or (330) 821-7363.

■ The Premier Collar, Premier Pet Products, Richmond, VA; phone (804) 379-4702. Also available at most pet supply stores; about $7.
■ The Check Choke, Coastal Pet Products, Inc., Alliance, OH; available at pet supply stores; about $10.
■ The Lupine Combo Collar, Lupine Company, Conway, NH; phone (800) 228-9653l; about $8.
■ The Safe-T-Bright Collar, The Dogís Outfitter, Hazelton, PA; phone (800) 367-3647; about $5.
■ The Handler Dog Collar, UPCO, St. Joseph, MO; phone (800) 254-8726; $50
■ The Hand-E-Lead, The Dogís Outfitter, Hazleton, PA; phone (800) 367-3647; about $10.
■ The Scruffy Guider, Misty Pines Dog Park Company, Sewickly, PA; phone (412) 364-4122; www.mistypinesdogpark.com; $24.95 plus shipping and handling.

Books

The Complete Idiot's Guide to Labrador Retrievers, Joel Walton and Eve Adamson, Howell Book House/Alpha Books, 1999; softcover, 300pp., $16.95, ISBN 1-58245-030-7.

This book is jam-packed with information invaluable to owners of all breeds of dogs, not just Labradors. The book is non-technical, exceptionally readable, and offers a step-by-step training guide that uses positive training methods. It also includes excellent tips on maintaining your dog's health; down-to-earth advice on all aspects of dog care, nutrition, exercise, and grooming; and an extensive resource list.

Dogs Are From Neptune, Jean Donaldson, Lasar Multimedia Productions, 1998; softcover, 162 pp., $14.95; ISBN 0-9684207-1-0.

This book consists of Donaldson's answers to questions asked by dog owners with dog behavior problems, with heavy emphasis on aggression. It is written with Donaldson's trademark engaging, humorous language, and contains a wealth of information based on positive training methods.

Unfortunately, the Q&A format of the book necessarily interrupts the flow of the writing, hence the final product is not as captivating as her former book, *Culture Clash* (ISBN 1-888-047-05-04). If you are a Donaldson fan you will love it. If you have a dog with aggression problems or are simply interested in acquiring more information on canine behavior problem resolution, this book is a great addition to your library.

Running With the Big Dogs: The Gentle Art of Turning Your Retired Racing Greyhound into Your Best Friend, Lee Livingood, self-published, 1998; softcover, 129 pp., $26; No ISBN #, available for purchase from Lee Livingood at lcl@paonline.com

This book is an excellent resource for anyone interested in rescuing one or more of the victims of the greyhound racing industry. Each year more than 25,000 dogs are retired from the track.This book covers in detail how to decide whether a greyhound is for you, how to find and select the right dog, helping him adapt to life as a companion animal, and basic training, using very positive methods.

The Irrepressible Toy Dog, Darlene Arden, Howell Books, 1998; hardcover, 177 pp., $17.95; ISBN 0-87605-649-4

Darlene Arden knows her subject – this book is laden with information about the raising and keeping of toy dogs. She incorporates some current thinking on positive reinforcement and clicker training, but is too quick, in our opinion, to counsel the use of an aversive "No!" for puppies. We also disagree with her position on "tug-of-war." While Arden falls in the "tug-of-war-makes-them-aggressive" camp, we believe that tug-of war can be a very useful training tool if done properly.

The extensive section on diseases will be useful to toy dog owners, and much of the other information is good, such as the warning to owners of small dogs to be sure to put them down occasionally and encourage them to be dogs, not just lap ornaments.

Bandit: Dossier of a Dangerous Dog, Vicki Hearne, Harper Collins,1991. *Bandit* recounts Hearne's efforts to save a remarkable dog sentenced to death for biting. The case, widely publicized at the time, revolved around the furor over the almost universal perception of "pit bulls" as an inherently dangerous breed.

Clicker Training

Clicker Training Start-Up Kit, Karen Pryor (includes booklet and clickers), Sunshine Books, 1-800-47-CLICK.

Clicker Training for Obedience Competition: Shaping Top Performance—Positively!, Morgan Spector, Sunshine Books, 1-800-47-CLICK. This book offers step-by-step clicker-training tips for people training either obedience competitors or family companions.

Clicker Training for Obedience, Morgan Spector, Sunshine Books, 1999; softcover, 267 pp., $29.95; ISBN 0-9624017-8-1

This is a great choice for the serious obedience competitor on your gift list who wants to maintain a positive relationship with her dog based on partnership and cooperation rather than punishment and intimidation, and still be in the running for those perfect 200 obedience scores. Spector's book dispels the myth that you can't use food to train "serious" and reliable dog behaviors. The author says of clicker training, "The dog comes to do what you want it to do. Reliability is almost 'built in' if the training is done properly." This book is a must-have for the competitor, as well as a good read for any dog owner interested in positive training methods.

WWW: Clicker training on the Web: www.clickertraining.com.

Videos

Sirius Puppy Training, Dr. Ian Dunbar, (90 min., $21.95.) This tape is a must-have for the family that has recently acquired a new puppy or is thinking about getting one. Dunbar was one of the pioneers of reward-based dog training in the U.S., and is the founder of the Association of Pet Dog Trainers, which promotes humane methods of dog training and ongoing education for dog trainers. His puppy training tape is chock-full of entertaining demonstrations of real-life puppy training, handling, and gentling, and emphasizes the importance of family participation in the training process. He includes invaluable information on how to prevent behavior problems such as biting, barking and housesoiling.

Clicker Magic, Karen Pryor, (56 min., $39.95. This video is a delightful collection of actual clicker-training sessions, some with Pryor, some with other trainers. "Clicker training" is a popular term for reward-based training that uses a "marker signal" – a clicker or other sound or word such as "Yes!" – that marks the instant of good behavior in the subject animal. The marker signal is followed by a reward such as food, praise, or play. *Clicker Magic* is a valuable addition to the library of any dog owner or trainer who is pursuing more positive methods of communicating with and training their canine companions.

Take a Bow—WOW!, Virginia Broitman & Sherri Lippman, (34 min., $24.95). This professionally produced tape emphasizes the importance of having fun with your dog when you train, and will show you how to use positive reinforcement methods to teach behaviors such as take a bow, play dead, ring a bell, roll over, open and more.

Bow WOW, Take 2, Virginia Boitman (38 min., $24.95)

Dancing With Your Dog: Tape 1: *Getting Started*, Sandra Davis (55 min., $29.95). Musical canine freestyle, or dancing with your dog combines basic training exercises such as heel, sit and lie down, with a series of flashier moves choreographed into a routine by the individual dog owner. It is captivating to watch, and addicting to participate in. Davis' video shows you how to get started in a step-by-step positive approach, and teaches you the secrets behind 20 movements that you can use in your dance routine. If you are bored with heeling in circles and want something fun and challenging to try, watch this video, then put on your dancin' shoes!

Dancing with Your Dog: Tape 2, *Getting the Rhythm*, Sandra Davis (55 min., $29.95). *Dancing With Your Dog*: Tape 3, *Getting Applause,* Sandra Davis (52 min., $29.95).

Freestyle videotapes:: Pat Ventre, Ventre Advertising, Inc., P.O. Box 350122, Brooklyn, NY 11235; (718) 332-8336

Dogs, Cats & Kids, by Dr. Wayne Hunthausen, (30 min., $19.95); Animal Behavior Consultations, 913-362-2512. An excellent video featuring pet behavior specialist Wayne Hunthausen, DVM, which should be required viewing for all families with kids. The entertaining tape teaches children (and adults) the correct way to approach and handle pets, how to read body language, when to leave an animal alone, and what to do about strays. It succeeds in instilling respect for animals without creating fear. The lessons contained are ones that every child needs to learn in order to be safe around dogs and cats.

*"Paw-sitive" Dog Training, (*106 min., $29.95}; Allan Bauman/Goldenbrook Kennels, Direct Book Services, 800-776-2665. Allan Bauman is owner/trainer of Goldenbrook Kennels in Wooster, Ohio, and President of the Association of Pet Dog Trainers. Bauman's video shows how to use lure and reward methods effectively to teach basic training exercises. He uses untrained dogs and puppies in the video and gives convincing demonstrations of how quickly and well gentle luring methods can work.

Click and Treat Training Kit, by Gary Wilkes, (55 min., $49.95). *Patient Like the Chipmunks*, Robert Bailey & Marian Breland-Bailey, (45 min., $49.95).

Training Dogs with Dunbar, Dr. Ian Dunbar, (65 min., $34.95).

Training Dogs. John Fischer (60 min, $21.95).

Training the Dog in the Human Pack, John Fischer (60 min., $21.95)

Highlight Tapes

1997 Second Pup-Peroni Canine Freestyle Championship, $40, Ventre Advertising, Inc., 718-332-8336. Routines from simple to spectacular, with dogs performing moves you thought only possible through computer simulation.
'97 World Frisbee Finals (45 min., $19.95). The 16 dogs featured demonstrate astounding athletic ability. Heavily dominated by herding breeds – border collies and Australian shepherds– these dogs flip, spin, vault, and leap their way through Freeflight routines and Mini-Distance competitions.

1994 & 1995 World Dog Shows Dog Agility Highlights, (88 min., $30.95). If you are an agility enthusiast and want to see top agility dogs totally engaged in their sport, this a great tape for you.

Building a Better Flyball Dog, Scott Lucken (80 min., $40, J&J Dog Supplies, 800-642-2050). Starts out well with thrilling footage of flyball teams racing, jumping hurdles, grabbing the ball and racing back over the hurdles. But the video starts to drag as trainer/narrator Scott Lucken plods through several repetitions of each step in the flyball training process. However, the training methods Lucken offers seem sound and are based in positive reinforcement.

Clicker Training

Click & Go: Clicker Fun With Dr. Deborah Jones (33 min., $20.25). 1999, Deborah Jones/Planet K-9, Canine Training Systems, 303- 973-2107; http://www.caninetraining.com. Wow! This is the best dog training clicker video we have seen yet. Deborah Jones is a psychologist, behaviorist, Board member for the Association of Pet Dog Trainers (APDT, which promotes positive, dog-friendly training methods), and owner/trainer for Planet K9 in Dayton, OH. Jones provides a brief, engaging history of positive training methods, and explains and demonstrates the difference between shaping, luring and targeting. She moves on to basic training exercises, using short verbal explanations followed by hands-on demonstrations with happy dogs who are eager to show off their abilities.

Click & Fetch: Clicker Fun With Dr. Deborah Jones, 35 min., $29.95 1999, Deborah Jones/Planet K-9, Canine Training Systems, 303- 973-2107; http://www.caninetraining.com. Deborah Jones comes to the rescue of every dog owner—and every dog—who has been dismayed by a trainer's insistence that a forced retrieve can only be taught through the painful ear-pinch or other coercive method. After reprising some basic information presented in Jones' first video, this one shows how to shape a retrieve using methods that work with the most to the least motivated canine.

Frisbee Dogs (30 minutes, $24.95); Peter Bloeme, PRB & Associates, Inc., 404-231-9240 One of the nice things about Frisbee for dogs is that they generally love it so much that the activity is its own reward. Frisbee dogs are wildly enthusiastic about the sport, and no one suggests jerking them with a choke chain or zapping them with a shock collar to get them to chase a flying disc. The video also promotes shelter adoptions, teaches owners how to throw the disc, demonstrates a variety of grips and throws, explains how to motivate an unenthusiastic Frisbee student (canine), and a "health and hazard advisory."

Toys

Rubber Tug Toys

Cressite Solid Rubber Tug Toy, Pet Supply Imports, Inc., South Holland, IL (made in England) $7.79. Available at most pet stores. The Cressite Rubber Tug Toy is made of natural rubber and was very inviting to our test dogs. The price is reasonable, but given the somewhat flimsy construction, reserve this toy for dogs 25 pounds and under.

Four Paws Rough & Rugged, Four Paws Products, Ltd., Hauppauge, NY (made in China); $12.99. Available at most pet stores. Rough & Rugged gets the rubber toy vote, paws down. It is also made of natural rubber, and is more than twice the thickness of the Cressite Tug Toy, which increase its durability substantially. It is a decent length to separate hands from jaws (13 inches), which should give Rambo the needed distance to differentiate rubber from skin.

Tennis Ball Toys

Cassidy Big Tug/D, Farlar Int'l., Camarillo, CA. (made in USA);.$14.99. Available in pet stores. This tug toy has a tennis ball securely attached to two ropes at one end of the toy. A full 22 inches away, a rubber handle encircles the rope, making it easy for the owner to hold on to the toy – and win the game! Rambo has plenty of room to chomp the ball or the rope, without getting too close to human skin at the handle end. This is the kind of toy that would be most useful to teach the rules of "Tug 'o War" to your dog.

Braided Rope Toys

Dogs love to chew these colorful, heavy, cotton braided ropes for hours – which is exactly the problem; when swallowed, the tiny threads can wreak havoc in the intestines, sometimes necessitating surgery. As a tug toy, though, they can be great. Just don't leave them lying around – they should always be put away at the end of the game.

Booda Wonder Tug (Twin), Aspen Pet Products, Inc. Denver, CO, $15.49. Available at most pet stores. Comes with all the extras you need for a really safe tug toy with a larger dog. A soft rubber handle protects the owner's hand, some 27 inches from the business end of Rambo's teeth. Halfway down the rope the toy splits into two ends, giving Rambo a choice if he tends to bounce around with his teeth.

.

Floatable Frisbee™, Nylabone Products, Neptune, NJ; 800-631-2188, ext. 108; $8.95. The Floatable Frisbee closely resembles the beloved plastic Frisbee flying disc. It is shaped like one, flies almost as well as one, (unlike many of the canine flying disc toys, and has several improvements over the original. It is made of a soft, durable rubbery material (safer for the dog and suitable even for gentle indoor play), and has a raised bone built into the top for easy pick-up. Ignore the part of the accompanying instruction booklet that discusses the maker's suggestions on how to teach the forced retrieve; it's not a method we would ever approve of.

"Softflex" Clutch Ball, Hueter Toledo Co., Inc., Bellevue, OH; $9.99; Available from pet stores and catalogs; also Valley Vet Supply, 800-360-4838. This quickly became the most sought-after toy for fetching and chewing. It's not intended as a chew toy, and probably wouldn't hold up to serious gnawing, but the soft, rubbery material takes lots of bites and punctures without splitting. The surface of the Clutch Ball is not smooth,, but formed with easily grabbed indentations, making it easy for any dog to carry it. Best yet, when used as a fetch toy, it's so soft that it can't hurt any dog if accidently "conked" on the head or caught in mid-air with the teeth.

Index